How To G
Not Lose

Dealing With the Physical and
Emotional Challenges of Sight Loss

A guide for families, friends,
care providers, and people losing their sight.

R. Mike Harmer

Since 1978

PO Box 221974 Anchorage, Alaska 99522-1974

ISBN 1-59433-034-4

Library of Congress Catalog
Card Number: 2005928764

Copyright 2005 by R. Mike Harmer
—First Edition—

Manufactured in the United States of America.

Dedication

Dedicated to all individuals and agencies providing services to enable blind and visually impaired people to lead productive and happy lives. To say that your efforts are appreciated would be a huge understatement.

Acknowledgments

I would love to mention everyone who has touched my life, as each has influenced my ability to deal with my vision loss and helped me to become the person I am today. The list would be too long and frankly, my memory is not that good. My life as it is today, started the day of my diagnoses with an incurable eye disease. So many fine people and organizations have helped me deal with my vision loss, that I am sure I will miss someone. If so, it was not intentional.

I thank Boyd Walker, OD, for detecting my eye disease and getting me to see Dr. Tom Harrison, MD and Dr. David Swanson, MD, who made the diagnosis. Doctor Swanson provided some of the information for this book, as well.

My rehabilitation started with the Homer Independent Living Center, the Alaska Department of Vocational Rehabilitation, and a small support group, formed by John Clare. Mary Huffnagle and Debbie Grimes were a big help.

I cannot say enough good things about the US Department of Veterans Affairs Blind Rehabilitation Center at American Lake in Washington

State. The entire staff is my heroes. I recovered much of my self-confidence here. I thank Glenn Buttkus and Irene Yang, OD, for their help, friendship and encouragement. I owe a big debt of gratitude to Martha Farris for getting me there.

The writers group known as Invisible Ink has been a constant source of encouragement during the writing of this book. I received enthusiastic encouragement from many sources, including most of the above-mentioned folks. I have enjoyed working with the Homer V.I.P.'s (Visually Impaired Persons), a low vision support group. Thanks to Angela Elling for her time and effort. The always positive and cheerful attitude of Dave Luck has been inspirational.

I extend my gratitude to John Clare, Angela Elling, Bonnie Schneider, and Doctor David Swanson, MD for reading the finished manuscript. I appreciate your comments and suggestions. I have incorporated your suggestions into the finished work.

My own personal support group, my family and friends have been a constant source of help and strength. You will never know how much help you have been.

My wife, Gwen, always a pillar of strength, has kept me from drowning in the depression pit and has never complained about my lack of attention to her as I threw myself into the writing of this book.

Thanks to my wife, my son Gordon, daughter-in-law Tina, and a great staff, I was able to keep my business in operation until I decided it was time to retire. This was truly a great team effort.

My daughter Karen, who lives in Canada, has also been a positive influence. Her stick-to-it attitude and determination to do a good job and complete the task, helped keep me going when I started to run out of the enthusiasm required to complete this book. Hang in there; "good things happen to good people."

I thank everyone who contributed in one way or another.

Contents

Introduction

Losing your sight and learning to live with reduced or even no vision is a major event, and one that we do not plan on happening to us. Unfortunately, according to the National Eye Institute, approximately 130,000 Americans will be afflicted with blindness or a visual impairment this year. The vast majority of these will be from one of four major eye diseases, and others from injury. It happened to me. This book is about *How To Go Blind And Not Lose Your Mind*. It is about keeping a proper perspective and how to deal with the physical and emotional problems of sight loss. Your vision of your future need not be tossed into the trash.

On a trip to my local library, I could find no book that would help prepare me to deal with my vision loss. I thought that there should be. This book is the one that I had been looking for. If you or a loved one is in the process of sight loss, this book could be of help. It should make living with low vision a little easier.

I am not a low vision specialist, or a doctor. I am not an expert at anything. I am merely an ordinary person, who has learned to live with low vision.

I would like to share what I have learned in the hope that it will make life a little easier for someone else who may be losing his or her sight.

Losing your sight is not an easy thing to accept, but it does not have to be hard. It can happen rapidly or slowly, and it can happen to anyone. How you deal with it will not only affect you, but also those around you. It can be an interesting side trip on this road we call life, and it can be scary without a map. If you are reading this book, then you are on the right road.

Chapter 1
The Diagnosis

Going blind is easy. Anyone can do it. Blindness does not discriminate by age, sex religion, nationality or race. It is an equal opportunity condition, and one that few of us have to deal with. When confronted with this enormously serious situation, we will need help in dealing with the physical and emotional challenges ahead. There are no instruction books on how to go blind. I know, because after I received a diagnosis of an incurable eye disease that had no known cause or no known cure, I tried to find one. I will not kid you; I was more than just a little concerned when informed that I would probably lose a lot of my central vision. Central vision is what we see directly in front of us. It would be an understatement to say that it is important that we have it. There was a time when I would have said that it was vital to our existence, although I do not feel that way now.

After my diagnosis, I was certain that I would have a lot of work ahead of me, particularly after looking for and not finding information to help me deal with it. Little did I know how much time and effort I would have to put in to cope with the new development in my life, and one that would be changing my life and my family's life in many, many ways.

By now, you have probably already been to see an ophthalmologist. I am writing this book under the premise that your doctor has diagnosed your eye problem as an eye disease, and informed you that you may lose some or all of your sight, or perhaps you have an eye disease or injury that has already taken some or all of your sight. *How To Go Blind And Not Lose Your Mind* should be beneficial in either case.

A major event has occurred. Your life is about to change in many ways. It took me longer than I believe it should have to realize this. Once I had realized this and accepted that there would have to be some major changes in the way I did things, life got a lot easier. At this point, you are probably still in shock and wondering why such a thing is happening to you.

Before I go further, I suggest you obtain a second opinion. Even if your eye doctor is the best in the world, I feel it is important to get a second opinion. If you do not, there could very well be a time in the future that you may wonder, "what if I had only…" (obtained another diagnosis). This is strictly for your own benefit. You will feel better knowing that you have left no stone unturned. There will be no question in your mind that there may have been a treatment for your particular eye disease, or even a possibility that it was an entirely different problem. It is not a matter of not having confidence in your doctor.

In fact, he or she may have already suggested you get a second opinion.

If your doctor had to tell you that you would be losing some or all of your sight (otherwise having to tell you that you are going blind), it was not done lightly. I discussed this with one of the eye doctors who had to give me the bad news. He told me that it was not any easier telling someone this now than it was 20 years ago. He said that the doctor must somehow present overwhelmingly bad news with truth, compassion, and a message of hope. He said that a patients reaction to bad news varies tremendously, depending on many factors such as age, level of education, cultural background, previous illness, other encounters with the health care system, family obligations or support, plans for the future, etc., but it seems that most people eventually learn to cope with their loss. He said that it was interesting that young males who incur a serious injury to only one eye require an average of two years before they are able to return to the work force. The loss of self-image and physical function, especially in that population, is extremely difficult to overcome.

Regardless of how your doctor presented the diagnosis to you, and how well you think that you have taken it, I imagine that you are in some stage of shock. No matter how calm, cool, and collected you may think you are, news of this magnitude sometimes takes a little time to soak in. In my case, I do not think it really sank in until it was noticeable that I actually was losing sight. I believe I really did not think it would happen, or perhaps some type of a miracle would intervene. Well, no miracles came along. Let me tell you a little about what happened to me after my diagnosis, and how the idea for this book came about.

The idea for *How To Go Blind And Not Lose Your Mind* or at least the need for a book like this germinated gradually over a five or six-year period after a diagnosis of an eye disease, as I was told, "had no known cause and no known cure" and I would be losing a significant portion of my central vision. After having enjoyed near perfect vision for all of my 57 years, this was a chilling thing to hear. Well, they were correct. My visual acuity at the time was 20/20 without correction. Within five years, it dropped to 20/800.

My vision loss was rapid during the first two years. In a little under 18 months, I had to discontinue driving after my visual acuity dropped to below the legal driving requirement of better than 20/40. In 24 months, I became legally blind when my visual acuity had dropped to 20/200 in one eye, and 20/300 in the other. What do these numbers mean? When a person has 20/200 it means they can see at 20 feet what a person with normal vision (20/20) can see at 200 feet. Losing even 50 feet can be a big change.

As of this writing, eight years has elapsed since it had been determined that my eyes had a particularly bad type of a common eye disease called macular degeneration, an eye disease that is the leading cause of blindness in the United States than any other eye disease. I had never heard of it. The only eye disease that I had ever heard of is glaucoma. My father had this and I came down with it seven years prior to the arrival of macular degeneration into my life. Although I am not going to spend time discussing the various eye diseases, and there are several, I will discuss macular degeneration. I am doing so, because it is the leading cause of blindness in the United States. This eye disease has also taken a good-sized piece of my sight. This should also aid in your understanding of what I have had to deal with and as well, what you may have to deal with. While I do have another eye disease called glaucoma, macular degeneration is what has done the damage to my eyes. The glaucoma was first, but its progression stopped with medication, thanks to the early detection of the disease. Macular degeneration had no treatment at the time of my diagnosis. Since then, a treatment that will slow or perhaps even stop the progression of the "wet" type of macular degeneration is available. Perhaps I should start here.

First, the correct term is "age related macular degeneration," or AMD. It is called age related, because it normally happens to people over the age of 55. AMD gradually destroys sharp central vision. We use central vision to see objects clearly and for common daily tasks such as reading, writing, and driving. It also allows you to recognize faces of friends and family members. In some people, AMD advances so slowly that it will have little effect on their vision as they age. In others, the disease progresses faster and may lead to a loss of vision in one or both eyes. You may wonder just how AMD damages vision. Let me explain.

The retina is a paper-thin tissue that lines the back of the eye and sends signals to the brain. In the middle of the retina, a tiny area called the macula is located. The macula is composed of millions of tiny light-sensing cells helping to produce central vision. Central vision is what we see directly in front of us, as opposed to peripheral vision, which is what we see to the sides while looking ahead. Glaucoma is an eye disease that takes the peripheral vision, which I will not get into here. AMD comes in two forms known as dry and wet AMD.

Ninety percent of all people with AMD have the dry type. Scientists are not sure what causes dry AMD. Studies suggest that an area of the retina becomes diseased leading to the slow breakdown of the light-sensing cells in the macula and a gradual loss of central vision.

Wet AMD affects only 10 percent of all people with AMD, although it accounts for 90% of all blindness from this disease. As dry AMD worsens, new tiny blood vessels may start to grow behind the retina and cause wet AMD. Because these new blood vessels are very fragile, they will often leak blood and fluid under the macula. This causes rapid damage to the macula and can lead to the loss of central vision in a relatively short period. This is the type I have. I did not have the dry type to start with. Instead, I went directly into the wet type. Apparently, mine was from heredity, although there is no known family history of it. Perhaps a bum gene decided to pick on me. People over the age of 60 are at greater risk. Whites are more likely to get it than blacks, and women more so than men. Those with a family history of this eye disease are at greater risk of developing the disease. Scientists believe smoking increases the risk as well. Although AMD can occur in middle age, studies show people over age 60 are at greater risk than other age groups. An early sign of dry AMD is blurred vision. Early signs of wet AMD are straight lines looking crooked. Although I have the wet type, I never noticed straight lines looking crooked. I did have blurred vision, but learned that it was from the leaking blood vessels. I guess that my disease did not know how to act. A small blind spot may also develop. There is no pain with either type.

There is currently no treatment for dry AMD, with the exception of vitamin therapy. This type of therapy should be under your ophthalmologists' recommendation and supervision. Some cases of wet AMD are treatable with laser surgery or drug therapy. This will slow or sometimes stop the disease from progressing. Early detection is essential for this. Lost vision is not restorable once it has been lost. I hope research will develop a way to restore lost sight one day. From what I have learned, gene therapy may one day be used. I have little or no knowledge in this area of medical science, although I intend to find out, if possible. I would try to be first in line to be a test subject for anything that looks hopeful.

Most of the information I have provided about macular degeneration has been from information furnished by the National Eye Institute. You can obtain information about your eye disease, or any others, from this fine source.

My vision loss was rapid during the first two years, and continued to deteriorate for another two to three years. Since then my sight has stabilized as the disease has become inactive. I am hoping it stays that way. Eye specialists tell me it will probably stay that way, but there is no guarantee. Apparently, there is a possibility it could become active again. My main concern at this point is to keep my glaucoma under control. If I lost my peripheral vision, I would be in deep trouble. I have come to depend on it, and I use it a lot, now that I am more aware of it. Peripheral vision is one of those things I never gave much thought to. Until I lost my central vision, I had not realized just how much I depended on it.

There are four major eye diseases. They are macular degeneration, glaucoma, diabetic retinopathy, and cataracts. There are many other lesser-known eye diseases that are every bit as destructive, if not more so. Blindness from any eye disease can be a tragic loss. I will not go into detail on other eye diseases, as there are books and other printed material on each of these diseases, written by doctors, scientists and low vision specialists who have the technical knowledge necessary to write on these subjects. I do not possess the technical knowledge to write such a book. There is a lot of information on these eye diseases from sources I will mention in this book.

If you have a computer and access to the internet, you can start investigating now. The internet is one of the sources of which I will be discussing.

The past eight years have been an interesting learning experience for me. At this time, I consider it an adventure.

Fear, frustration and irritation are just a few of the emotions you will probably have to deal with. You may also have feelings of helplessness and, at times, hopelessness. There was a period that I felt abandoned for a while. It was like waking up in the middle of the Pacific Ocean, and then having to paddle back to civilization without a compass. I did not know which direction to go.

As my sight went downhill, I found myself losing a lot of my independence. For a person who has been fiercely independent all of his life, this was a huge loss. My self-confidence and self-esteem were also taking a beating. This probably sounds like I was a wreck, and going downhill fast. I could have easily become a wreck if I had allowed it to happen.

At one point, I believe I had started to feel sorry for myself, something I had consciously been trying to avoid. I was sure that doing so would drag me down. Never the less, I started feeling abandoned and felt I would have to deal with losing my sight on my own. You see, once the doctors determined they could not fix my problem, they lost interest in me, or so I thought at the time. I paid my bill and went home to go blind. I went home with no idea of what kind of help might be available. I did not know where to start looking for help. I did not even know if I needed help to cope with losing my sight or living with reduced vision (also known as low vision). I did not even know exactly what my eye disease was or what to expect from it.

The only good news I received was that I would probably not lose all of my sight, which was welcome news. The word blind probably still lingers in the back of my mind, which is where it should stay if it has to stay at all.

After I received my diagnosis, which was more of a prognosis, than a diagnosis, I left the doctors office confused, bewildered, and a little scared. It seemed I was on my own and would have to deal with it myself. The ophthalmologist sure didn't offer any help, and little or no information.

I went to the local library in the town where I live. I wanted to find information that would help me determine what problems I would be facing, and obtain ideas on how to deal with losing my sight and living with little or no sight. I could find no books on the subject other than one book describing one particular eye disease. It was probably then that the idea for *How To Go Blind And Not Lose Your Mind* got its start, or as someone commented, "the seed was planted."

I must confess, for a while I was a little mad at the doctors who made the diagnosis for leaving me to fend for myself in dealing with my eye disease. This was dumb on my part. After all, they did not cause my eye disease, and it was not their fault they could not cure an incurable disease. Rehabilitation was not their responsibility. Rehabilitation is the job for people who have special training to help people like me (and you) to adjust to and live with low vision.

I still feel the doctors should have information available to assist their patients in finding sources of help, such as local or national low vision support groups, and/or the name of one or more low vision specialists who have the training to evaluate and recommend training or visual aids for people with a visual impairment. Very few of us have the training to cope with a disability. We do not expect things like this to happen to us. When it does, we need a little direction when entering into a completely new way of living for which we will have to adjust to.

Former President Franklin D. Roosevelt once said, "The only thing to fear is fear itself." This started making sense to me finally. I realized that most of the things I fear are because I do not understand them. I realized a few months into my eye disease that knowledge was going to be a big factor in dealing with this new and unexpected turn in my life. I became determined not to let this thing beat me. I would learn how to deal with it, and I would live a normal life, or what I consider normal. Easier said then done! My journey was just beginning, and what a trip it has been! Now you are starting your journey. You are not starting it alone. There are approximately 14 million Americans with a visual impairment, with an estimated additional 130,000 more joining these ranks annually, according to the National Eye Institute.

It is my hope *How To Go Blind And Not Lose Your Mind* will give you direction and help in dealing with your vision loss. Sometimes all we need is someone to point us in the right direction. Based on my personal experiences in dealing with my sight loss, I will try to provide information and observations, throughout this book, about some of the problems you may encounter. I will provide suggestions on dealing with them, and any hints that may help you live with low vision. I will also provide you with information on some of the various forms of help available to you and some ideas about the various available visual aids. There are numerous resources available to help visually impaired people, and there are many sources of visual aid devices from talking watches to video magnifiers.

I believe I have learned to deal with my vision loss and have gained some useful experience. You will probably encounter some of the problems, which I feel are roadblocks to progress. Frankly, I think the experience has made a better person of me. My journey into the world of the visually impaired has not been without a few problems, but for the most part has been relatively smooth. I have leaned many new and interesting things, and I have met many very fine people. Some of them were also losing their sight, or had already lost some or all of their sight. Others are people who help those of us with vision problems. These people give a lot of their time and heart to help others improve their quality of life and to regain or improve their personal independence. The support of my family, friends, and even total strangers has been gratifying and helpful beyond description. I appreciate the help, support, and encouragement given me, more than they can know. Sometimes words are not enough.

One of the harder things for me, was learning to accept help, and knowing when to ask for it. Perhaps it is just a guy thing, but I had always had a hard time asking anyone for help. Perhaps it was because asking for help was a sign of weakness. This was some faulty thinking. I acquired this belief during the time I was growing up. Nothing could be further from the truth. I now believe a person must have an inner strength, a little wisdom, and a big desire to live a happy and complete life. Besides, it just makes good sense to ask for help when you need it.

As your vision loss progresses, you will find yourself doing many different things, and doing many things differently. It is sometimes amazing to me how well we can adapt to new situations. I found myself doing things and getting tasks done, by doing them differently. No one trained me to do some of these tasks differently. I seemed to do them differently by instinct. There is a lot more in that muscle between our ears, than we give it credit. Do not underestimate your abilities. I believe we can do things we had no idea we could do.

One of the more beneficial things you can do

for yourself is to keep a positive, "can do" attitude. You will be able to accomplish more, and it will be more pleasant to you and those around you as you accomplish them. You are not the only victim of your eye disease. If you are married, your spouse will be a victim too, as well as your children and grandchildren, if you have any. Others affected, if you are still in the work force, are the people you work with. In fact, just about anyone with whom you have contact. Some will be affected more than others. Some may never realize it. It is a little like tossing a stone into a lake. It causes a ripple effect that goes far beyond where it entered the water.

Since your diagnosis, you have probably experienced some emotions you may not have known before. There will probably be more, and you will have to deal with them. You cannot ignore them. I will discuss these in the next chapter, and probably touch on them throughout this book.

Your doctor has made the diagnosis, and has probably told you something you did not want to hear. He or she told you what you needed to know and probably did not sugar coat the information you received about your condition. You did not ask to go on this journey, but here you are! You might as well enjoy the ride. You might as well get all you can from the experience. It can be an interesting learning experience, if you allow it. Losing your sight is not all bad news. There is a good side. I have actually found several benefits from being legally blind. If you look hard enough, you can find some good in just about anything. I will talk more about these benefits later in *How To Go Blind And Not Lose Your Mind.*

Every day is the first day of the rest of our life. On the day your doctor made the diagnosis of your eye disease, that day became the first day of the rest of your new life. Make the most of it!

If you dislike change, learning new things, and meeting new people, you could have a tough time dealing with your vision loss. Some people withdraw from family, friends, and activities they had enjoyed. They are unwilling to accept what is happening to them, and become shut-ins. Others refuse to admit they have a vision problem at all. Many of them continue to drive and pose a serious danger to others as well as to themselves. You cannot allow any of the above to happen to you. I will be discussing this more in future chapters.

Now that you have a diagnosis, it is time to get on with your life. Roll up your sleeves; it is time to get to work! What you do now will influence your quality of life and the way you will live with low vision, or even no vision. Do not feel sorry for yourself. Others can do this for you. Besides, it is a waste of time. You cannot waste any time now, particularly if your eye disease is a type that rapidly destroys your sight. You can handle it, and may even be able to keep one step ahead of its progression.

Chapter 2
After The Diagnosis

Okay, you have had your diagnosis, and the news you received was not what you wanted to hear. If the prognosis was that you are going to lose some or all of your sight, it was probable that it was not what you expected. It is likely you left your ophthalmologist bewildered, confused, and even a little scared. There is nothing wrong with this. It would be unusual if you were not.

The morning after I received my bad news, I was looking into the bathroom mirror, and I said to myself, *you are going blind, now what do you do?* I had no idea what to do. I had no idea as to how much sight I might lose, and I had no idea how rapidly I would lose it. Frankly, it took several weeks before I really did anything. I believe I thought it was not really going to happen. I was in denial. Other than a little blurry vision in one eye, I could see quite well. I had been in bad situations before, and things always seemed to work out. I had always been lucky that way, it seemed. Well, things did not get better, and I had wasted a lot of time waiting for a miracle, when I should have been facing reality and accepting what was happening to me.

It is now that you must be aware of the various emotions lurking and waiting to control your life. Be aware of them and know there are ways to combat them. I will review what I observed and what seemed to work to overcome them. I can look back on it now and remember what worked to alleviate some of the problems I had encountered. I could have prevented some of them. My hindsight is 20/20.

If you were lucky, your doctor was able to explain to you exactly what your eye disease is and what will likely happen. Your doctor would have given you a diagnosis and a prognosis. The diagnosis identifies the disease by examination, testing and analysis. The prognosis is a prediction of the course, and outcome of the disease. I hope you had someone with you to help take notes so you have some of the names and terms used by the doctor. You need this information to help you obtain a better understanding of your problem. If you did not get it all, or need some clarification, do not hesitate to call your doctor and get the information you need. I did not follow this advice, but came home with enough strange names and terms to get me started on my own research. Fortunately, I retained many of these unfamiliar names and terms, although much of what the doctor said went over my head, except for the word *blind*. I remembered that word. The word *blind*, an unwelcome word, became burned into my memory. This word lodged into my mind as soon as he said it. The doctor was talking about me! I thought I knew what the word meant. I have a much better Understanding of what it means now. Experience does that for you.

One of the first things you are going to have to do is to accept your problem for what it is and what it might do to you. Be honest with yourself, and stay away from the doom and gloom scenario. Negative thinking can only drag you down. Once you can accept what is happening to you, then you can move forward. This is why a second opinion is important. It will remove any lingering doubt in your mind and keep you away from the denial thing.

There are several things you can do to learn how to cope with your eye disease, but first you had better know what you are going to have to deal with. Go to your local library and find information on your specific eye disease. If you find that information is scarce, or difficult to locate, then ask a librarian for help. Explain your situation and your need for information about your eye disease. I have found that they will bend over backward to help. If the library does not have what you need, they can order it, if it is available.

In my opinion, the internet, known as the information highway, is probably the best available source of information. If you do not own a computer, I highly recommend you get one and learn how to use it for information gathering, communication via email, and word processing. Do not worry about not being able to see the monitor. There is equipment that will allow you to use a computer even if you should become completely blind. You can pick up a used one, often for a fraction of the cost of a new one. It should not be too difficult to find someone to help you find one. If you purchase a used one from a private party, it would be a good idea to take it to a reputable computer shop to get it checked over, and remove programs that may be of no use to you. They can check it and remove any virus which may have infected it. When your sight is to the point you cannot read what is on the monitor screen, there are computer magnification programs, such as one called Zoom-Text. It enlarges the images you are viewing on the screen. What you are viewing is enlargeable up to 16 times. You will need a larger monitor to handle the increased size. A 20-inch monitor will work fine, but in this case, bigger may be better. If you can obtain one, a 23-inch screen may work better, depending on the degree of your sight loss. There are other similar programs for sale, and probably for less money, but at the time of this writing, I believe Zoom-Text is one of the better programs, but it is the only one I have purchased. Any of them should be helpful. None of these programs are inexpensive, so be prepared for sticker shock.

Do not be worried if you do not know how to use a computer. I learned the basics with minimal training. I am not a computer whiz, and never will be, but I am functional. After having used one, I would be lost without the means to find information, and monitor new and ongoing research and development on eye diseases. Research laboratories and universities around the world are doing a tremendous amount of research into the various eye diseases. I have seen several major break-throughs just in the relatively short time I have had an interest in living with a visual impairment. There is every reason to be optimistic for new cures and new ways to deal with vision loss.

Another thing I recommend is that you try to locate a low vision support group in your area. You can check the yellow pages, your local librarian, or check the phone book for an Independent Living Center in your area. They should know if there is one. Support groups are a fine source of information and can give you the opportunity to talk with others who have experienced much of what you may be facing. They can give you ideas and tips on what might be of help to you. As well, they may have low vision devices you can look at and perhaps have an opportunity to try out. Finding out what may work, and what may not work, could save you a lot of time, frustration, and money.

There are also national support groups, and they can direct you to a local branch in your area. There are two large national organizations. One is the NFB, or National Federation of the Blind. The other is the American Foundation for the Blind (AFB). There are many other organizations than these, including some dedicated to specific eye diseases. You may find state and local chapters where you live. These organizations are a gold mine for information, and can direct you to sources and resources to help you deal with your vision loss.

I am staying away from statistics as much as possible. There are a lot of them, and statistics on a subject vary from one source to another. I have come to look on them as being estimates, or even educated guesses. For example, one organization says that approximately 10 million Americans are legally blind or have a vision impairment, while another says 14 million. While the numbers differ, the message is clear. There are a lot! By these numbers, you can see that you are not alone with your problem. Eye diseases and blindness resulting from them are probably greater than you could have ever imagined. I was amazed at the numbers when I started looking at them. It is not hard to find statistics if you are looking for them. The statistics I use are to help make a point. They are not necessarily accurate. If I am sure of their accuracy, I will say so.

As I previously mentioned, try not to feel sorry for yourself. The pit of self-pity can be bottomless. Once you fall in, it can be a tough job climbing back out.

There may be times when you feel helpless, and there could be a time when all seems hopeless. Watch out for depression if this happens. Depression will never be your friend. If you or a loved one observes any sign of depression, go see a doctor and tell him or her of your concern. Depression is easily treatable. If left untreated, it can lead to bigger problems. You really do not need more problems to deal with. Get if treated promptly. I was aware of this possibility from the onset. I tried hard not to let the situation get me down, but it still managed to sneak into my life. Fortunately, for me, my wife recognized the problem. I do not know if I was feeling helpless and/ or hopeless, which caused the depression, or vice-versa. It really makes little difference, as the result was the same in the end.

Chapter 3
Losing your Sight-What happens

Until you have a good understanding of your eye disease, you may very well be feeling a little bewildered and/or confused. You may even get mad and ask why this is happening to you. What did you do to deserve this terrible thing? Learning more about your eye disease will give you a greater understanding of your particular disease and why it happened (although some eye diseases have no known cause). You should also gain an understanding of what to expect as the disease progresses. As you learn more, you should find bewilderment and confusion evaporating. Knowledge, a powerful tool, will play an important part in your dealing with this new problem in your life. So, study and learn all you can about your eye disease. With this information, you will acquire knowledge allowing you to accept what has happened, and you will realize you have to do something about it. With acceptance, you can obtain the calmness and determination you will need to forge ahead. You can do it!

It was not your fault you are becoming visually impaired. You did not ask for it, but here it is. It is not going to go away and you are just going to have to accept and deal with it. Please be aware that you are not alone when it comes to sight loss. There are many sources of help available. This can come in the form of training to help you get around, identifying problem areas, and learning how to cope with them. Many types of visual aids are available from many sources. Magnifiers, large print dictionaries, computers you talk to and they perform tasks you tell it to do, books and magazines on tape you can listen to instead of reading, video reading machines, and many other useful devices that frankly, an entire book could be devoted to the subject. There is a wealth of personal help and low vision aids designed to help you keep your independence and quality of life enjoyable and comfortable.

I am walking you through the stages of sight loss, and suggesting what may happen. I am using my own experiences and observations as a guide. I am using the scenario that your eye disease is progressing somewhat gradually, as opposed to a few weeks, or less. I realize some diseases progress more rapidly than others and vary by individual. Mine took about 18 months to reduce my visual acuity from 20/20 to 20/200 (legal blindness). This was slow enough to give me time to adjust and find ways to deal with my diminishing sight. At the time, however, it seemed rapid as I frantically raced around searching for help and information. The passing of time can be a direct result of the situation people may find themselves. As I once read somewhere, "the length of a minute is determined by which side of the bathroom door you are on".

Your doctor is probably the only person who can give you any kind of an idea about how rapid your sight loss will be, and that will probably be an educated guess based on his or her knowledge and experience. I hope your sight loss will be gradual and gives you the time to adjust, as your visual acuity diminishes. I found it was not so bad, and was physically painless. You are not the first person to lose their sight, and you will not be the last. My doctor told me that most blind people have some sight. In my information search, I found statistics that said approximately 90% of all legally blind people have some degree of sight. Now, this is good news, is it not? I thought so when my doctor told me this. My visual acuity is at 20/800 and I can see most things. Granted, I cannot see anything clearly, but I have sight, and I am grateful for all of the sight I have. I certainly have a greater appreciation for the good sight I once had and took for granted. I believe we all take for granted the basic senses with which most of us come equipped. Sight, hearing, touch, smell, and taste are something we expect we will always have. When we lose part or all of any of these senses, it dawns on us how much we use and depend on them.

As your sight goes downhill, you will start needing and using magnifiers. The lower power magnifiers are larger in diameter and preferable to use initially. They will cover a larger area. These are sometimes called reading magnifiers and can be obtained in two and four power magnification. They can be located at drug stores, office supply stores, optometrist offices, and sometimes bookstores. You will find them labeled 2X and 4X. Eventually, you will require higher magnification. You will find that as you obtain higher strength magnifiers, the viewing glass gets smaller in diameter and thicker. This is because that in order to get more magnification, there has to be more curvature in the glass. This requires more glass. If you could get a high-powered magnifier with a large viewing glass in the unit, it would be too large and heavy, and you would not be able to hold it. It might not only be too heavy to hold, but even too heavy to lift.

As your sight diminishes, you will notice that you will require more light to read. As well, you will begin to need more contrast to read easier. You may find that it is easier to read black on a white, or white on a black background. You may find that different color print, or a different color background may make it easier to read the print. Many like black print on yellow paper. Someone sent me a letter with blue print on a blue background. It might as well have been a piece of blank paper, as I could not see the print. For me, I find black on white paper is easier to see under magnification.

For some, larger print may be useful. There are several large print publications available, although you may have to ask for them. I have seen a few magazines, including *Readers Digest* and *New York Times* in large print. I have even seen a large print newspaper in my ophthalmologists' office. I do not remember the name, but believe it was a weekly rather than a daily paper. There are also games and puzzle magazines in large print. If you have a newsstand or bookstore in your area, they should be able to help you obtain them. The large print publications will work until your acuity cannot handle it anymore. With a little luck, perhaps your vision loss will stop at this point, or maybe it is past this point now.

There are illuminated magnifiers that can help you to read and see smaller objects and print. These are hand held illuminated magnifiers, and work well for small jobs. They are handy to read price tags, medicine containers and labels, or to read instructions, ingredients, and such. They are also useful with which to look at small objects. Perhaps to see if a screw has a Phillips head or slot top so that you can determine what type of screwdriver to use. There are many more things that this hand held unit works well for. I carry one with me at all times. A newer rechargeable model is now available. I recommend getting it, if you decide to get one. If you do not, you will be buying many batteries. I had a bad habit of forgetting to turn the switch off. I had to buy and change the batteries constantly, which was an irritation and expense I could have done without. The newer rechargeable type turns on when you grasp it, and turns off when you release your grip on it. This feature will help pay for the additional cost of the unit. The rechargeable can operate for several weeks on one charge.

There are also desktop lights with magnifiers

that work well for light reading, or looking at documents. I would not want to read a book under one, however.

At some point, you will run out of useful magnifiers, or just plain get tired of them. Then it will be time to start investigating obtaining a video magnifier. This is a closed circuit television. The camera/magnifying device mounted on a stand, which is over a sliding table. Your reading material sits on the small table, which slides back and forth and up and down. Above it, but still part of the stand is a monitor or television where you can see the enlarged image of what you are looking at. They are available in black and white, or color. You can look at pictures, read, and even write under them. I have even read a complete book under mine. Libraries frequently have these available for folks with low vision.

There are also hand held models that plug into your television and project printed or other types of material onto the television screen. You are able to control the magnification level and focus. There are many brands and styles of these devices, known as a CCTV (closed circuit television). These are available at low vision specialty outlets. My visual acuity is at 20/800 and these units work well for me. There is a list at the back of this book listing some of the sources and resources. There are many low vision aids available. I will talk about them later. Be advised that the high tech devices can be expensive, but well worth the price if you really need one and can afford it. If you cannot afford something you really need to improve your quality of life, sources of help are available. This is where a support group can be helpful. Someone in the group may have what you need and can give you a demonstration. They usually can tell you where to locate the device, or perhaps they may have a device they have replaced with another, and would be willing to sell you their used unit at a price you could afford. It might be possible to borrow one. There are usually individuals, organizations, or government agencies that can assist you to locate and obtain devices or services that may help improve your quality of life. Do not be afraid to ask for help. Sometimes the only way to obtain help is to ask for it. Do not let misguided pride stop or slow you from living independently or productively. This is the voice of experience talking. At one point, I felt I was beating my head against the proverbial brick wall and getting nowhere. I finally got desperate, and began to look for help. I was amazed at the doors that opened and finding the help I needed to move on and get my life back on track. I am glad I took the extra effort to find some of the help I needed. It is not always easy to find.

I owned and managed a small business, which was starting to suffer from my vision problem. I was having a harder time dealing with my diminishing eyesight than I realized. Sales and profits were both falling, and I really did not know why. When I realized there were five families depending on my business for an income, I had a hard look at the problem. I found I was the problem. I had stopped creating new advertising material. I was reusing old ads, some of which were not very old. Originality became something someone else did. I also found I was avoiding customers, friends, and to a lesser degree, family and even the people I worked with every day. My business had been successful partly to good products, but I believe primarily because our customers received quality service and workmanship, and more importantly, there was a good person-to-person customer relationship. Most knew they were coming to a friendly and trustworthy business where honesty meant something.

Personal service was at the top of the list. I enjoyed knowing and helping my customers. They became my friends in addition to being my customers. As my eye disease progressed, I became less available to greet and help take care of their needs. They must have thought I was not interested in them anymore and began going elsewhere. They were not being served in the manner they had come to expect. They were human beings, and not just another dollar in the bank. The personal contact was missing. My self-confidence and self-esteem seemed to be missing as well.

I went to work on fixing the problem. I went to a local Independent Living Center for some suggestions on where to find help that would be useful to my business and me. They contacted our state department of vocational rehabilitation. This agency evaluated my problem and me. They then helped me obtain a computer and a program that enlarges what is on the monitor screen. I could actually see what was on the computer monitor.

They also found a person who could teach people with low vision to use a computer. I had also purchased a video magnifying machine (CCTV) to help me read and write. Some people call this type of device a reading machine. The device does not read to you, but magnifies the material under it to a size large enough to see. The device can enlarge standard newsprint up to 54 times the original size.

Armed with this equipment and training, my self-confidence began to return, and with it, some self-esteem. This helped me and gave me a reason to find even more help, if I could find it.

Private insurance rates had been rising rapidly, and premiums were becoming a financial burden. I could not afford to get sick or injured, and it would be too costly to die, so I had to find affordable health insurance for my wife and myself. As I found out, there is no such thing as affordable health insurance. I was in my 50s, so age was not helping anything.

One day I read in a newspaper that the president of my insurance carrier had received over a million-dollar bonus, just for doing the job she had been hired and paid to perform. Meanwhile, premiums continued rising at about 25% a year.

I decided that I would have to drop my own coverage. My wife and I could not afford insurance for the both of us.

I am a Navy veteran. A friend, who was also a veteran, suggested I make a phone call to our local regional Veterans Affairs office to see if I might have medical coverage from them. This turned out to be the best thing I could ever have done. I had never thought I was eligible, as I was a peacetime veteran, and I had thought only wartime veterans were covered. What a relief that was! The veteran's facility had a person who worked with blind and visually impaired veterans.

Not only would they look after my health care needs, but they also sent me to one of ten blind rehabilitation centers they operate across the US. I received seven weeks of quality training. They gave me training and sent me home with many useful low vision aids.

When I arrived home from training, I had recovered much of my self-confidence. I was able to resume working and the downward slide of my business slowed, eventually reversing the direction the business was heading. I had a lot of help and support from my family and staff as well as many great customers. As my visual problem started becoming known, I was pleasantly surprised at how many people were interested and concerned, and many were surprised I wanted to keep working and operating a business.

I could have given up and I would have been eligible for social security disability insurance, but I refused to give up. I enjoyed working. I enjoyed my business, and I liked my staff and my customers. I thought I had an obligation to my staff, my customers, and to my community. I also thought I owed it to myself not to give up. I know this probably sounds very old fashioned, and perhaps a little corny, but that is the way I feel. I cannot change even if I wanted to.

What I am trying to get across here, is that because you are losing your sight, you do not have to quit everything else. You don't have to lose your vision. You just are losing your sight, not your life. There will be things you cannot do, and things you probably should not do. For the most part, you should be able to do most of the things you have always enjoyed doing. You will have to change, or modify the way you do many things. You may have to learn a completely new way of doing some tasks.

I continued bowling as my sight went down-hill. Surprisingly, my bowling average continued to rise for a few years, until eventually leveling off. I still bowl to this day. As the bowling pins became harder to see, I had to change the way I bowl. I do not have a high average, but it is re-spectable. Very few bowlers in our league even know I am legally blind. This is all part of keep-ing much of your independence while living with low vision.

We have all experienced frustration during our life. Perhaps you have had a project going, or a repair job just would not come out the way it should. You then have to redo it, and redo it, and you still are unable to get the project completed or repaired the way it should. After a few (or sev-eral) unsuccessful tries, you start getting up tight about it and even a little mad. You are sure that what you are doing should work, but it just will not. We all have frustrations like this from time to time. I can just about guarantee that you will ex-perience many frustrations as you lose your sight.

There will be things you may have thought you could do with your eyes shut, and now you cannot. Simple tasks become difficult or even impossible to accomplish. You will probably become aware of how much you had used your sight to get something done. If you have been denying it, you may have to admit you now have low vision.

Do not panic if you cannot do something. Sometimes all you will need to do is to stop trying, take a deep breath, and think about it. Then try to figure out if there is another way to do it, or if perhaps, you are not doing it the right way. You may even have to sit down and read some directions or ask someone for help. Go ahead, Ask for help. You may not be able to see Slot B, into which Part A is supposed to fit. Heck, even with perfect sight you might not be able to make it fit.

You will probably become more aware of what you purchase in stores. A big red flag will rise inside your head when you see the words "some assembly required." If you have children, I am sure you are already aware of this danger sign. Even with perfect vision, those words can strike terror into the strongest, and smartest of people.

Just accepting that your sight loss will probably be permanent, is a positive step forward. You should be ready to accept some help, especially if you have been postponing it.

Chapter 4

Low Vision—What is it?

I have mentioned low vision several times. I think now would be a good time to explain just what low Vision is. I will give you the clinical description, a practical description, and then a description as seen though the eyes of a person who has been living with low vision for several years. In this case, they are my eyes.

The National Eye Institute provided a listing of visual acuity requirements a person must have to be considered to have low vision. The numbers came from organizations of ophthalmologists across the country. Their guidelines are quite varied. They responded with specific visual acuity values. To be considered to be a person with low vision, the numbers given were 20/30, 20/40, 20/50, 20/60, 20/70, 20/80, 20/100, 20/200, and even one at 20/400. Apparently, a person has to be legally blind to have low vision by the guidelines of two of the organizations. I will note here that legal blindness is 20/200 in the better eye. There would be no doubt that a person had low vision if legally blind.

While there is a big spread in visual acuity numbers to qualify as having low vision, there is a functional description, based on a person's ability to perform normal and routine tasks. Several sources, including the National Eye Institute and the Center for the Partially Sighted, use a similar description of low vision as "a visual impairment, not correctable by ordinary glasses, contact lenses, medicine, or surgery, which interferes with a person's ability to perform everyday activities like reading, writing, cooking, watching TV, shopping, etc." Otherwise, activities most take for granted.

These are all good methods to determine that a person has low vision, but, as seen through the eyes of a person with low vision, specifically, my low vision, the definition of low being used here means less than normal. As vision refers to sight, I am talking about a person who cannot see things as well as a person with normal vision.

Normal vision is having a corrected visual acuity of 20/20. A person with a visual acuity of less than 20/40 cannot obtain a drivers license in most, if not all 50 states. What do these numbers mean? For example: a person with 20/70 visual acuity can only see at 20 feet what a person with 20/20 visual acuity can see at 70 feet.

If I was to place a numerical visual acuity standard for low vision, I would establish it at 20/30 or 20/40. By the time ones visual acuity has dropped to that level, the ability to read small print is diminishing. Road signs become more difficult to read at a distance. Mine certainly was. Driving at night was becoming more of a challenge. I do not know what my visual acuity was when I took myself off the road as a driver, but it must have been worse than 20/50. It was not long after I stopped driving that I was tested to have 20/100 visual acuity. I know now that I should have quit driving much earlier, but I was fighting it. I knew when I would have to stop driving, that I would lose a lot of my personal independence. It was foolish of me to keep driving as long as I did, as I was endangering others as well as myself.

If you drive a vehicle, you too will have to make that decision at some point. You will know when. It is when you start feeling uncomfortable driving. That little voice in your head will tell you. Listen to it and do not put it off. I really had a sense of relief after I quit. I did not have to worry any longer about getting into an accident and injuring or even killing someone. I wish my doctor had tapped me on the shoulder and suggested I think about not driving, or even just flat out told me it was time to quit. However, it was my responsibility and I should have had enough good sense to do it. There is a point where there is a fine line between stupid and crazy. I believe I achieved both by not getting out from behind the steering wheel sooner. It was certainly stupid and crazy to have not done so sooner. Do not follow my example. Ask your eye care professional to keep an eye on your visual acuity and tell you when its time to hang up the keys. Do not fight it. Get your transportation system set up, and take yourself off the road. Yes, it will be a tough thing to do, but believe me; you will feel better for doing so. Peace of mind is the reward.

For me, low vision means seeing the newspaper but not the words on it or seeing a tree move in the breeze, but not the leaves. For me it means looking at the bay and not seeing the boats on it, or hearing a plane overhead and not being able to see it. For me it also means being able to see my hand at the end of my outstretched arm, but not the face of a friend on the other side of it.

Low vision may come to mean irritation, frustration, inconvenience and probably a whole lot more. It does not mean give up, quit trying or stop dreaming. You are going to be surprised at what you can do and how well you can adapt.

I also would recommend you try to locate a Blind Rehabilitation Center in your state, and apply for admission. You do not have to be completely blind to qualify. You can obtain valuable training that will increase your independence and quality of life. It can help restore self-confidence and self-esteem.

If you are a veteran, it would be wise to get into one of the VA operated Blind Rehabilitation Centers. They will be more cost effective and the quality of training is excellent. You may only have to pay the transportation expense to get there and back. Staffed by well-trained personnel, they have the facilities and equipment to give good training. You do not have to be a war veteran. Peacetime veterans are welcome, as I was.

At the time I went to the blind rehabilitation center for my training, I thought I was getting along quite well. I did not think I would learn anything useful I already did not know. I can only say I was very, very wrong. What I came home with was most of the tools to get my life back on track and join the human race once again. I have nothing but praise for the Department of Veterans Affairs Health Care System.

It is likely someone will ask you, as I was (several times), about your other senses improving. I have discussed this with low vision specialists and was told that no, your other senses (touch, hearing, taste, and smell) do not improve, but you start using them more efficiently. I found I was using my sense of touch (tactile senses) more, and had started using them early on into my vision loss. I had done so without realizing it.

I became aware of my increased use of my sense of touch when I was in blind rehabilitation training. My training started with tasks, which required using tactile senses. This continued throughout my training. I am more aware now, of how much I do use them, and depend on them to accomplish various tasks. I am sure you will too.

I cannot say if I am using the other senses more than I used to, or not. If I am, then I am not aware of it. It would be nice, however, if my "good sense" would improve. I still do some dumb things. If being smart was a prerequisite for going blind, I would still have 20/20.

Another fallacy is that losing your sight is a natural part of aging. With the exception of cataracts, this is not so. People over the age of 60 are at greater risk of eye disease, but age does not cause an eye disease to happen. Our eyes weaken as we age, which is why we need corrective glasses.

They are like little muscles that are always working. They have to work to let more light in or less light in, and are constantly busy focusing on all we see. We do not treat them very well, for the most part. We make them work in poor lighting, and then turn around and blast them with strong UV rays from the sun by not protecting them with sunglasses. We stick them, poke them, put dirt and other things into them, rub them, and we do not nourish them properly. It is no wonder they get tired and need a little help.

There is nothing normal about having an eye disease. Some of us may have a genetic predisposition to an eye disease. My father had glaucoma, so it was not a great surprise that I developed it when I was 50 years old. This happened seven years prior to the time when macular degeneration began. The glaucoma, detected early thanks to a routine eye exam, was treatable with medication. I was fortunate; it prevented the disease from developing further. I use medication in the form of eye drops and will have to use them for the rest of my life or until a permanent treatment is developed, and I am confident that one day there will be one found.

The macular degeneration that developed seven years later was a big surprise. There was no family history of it, at least for four generations, which is as far back as I was able to find information. Perhaps it was from an old dormant gene that decided to rear its ugly head. As there is no known cause for either disease, I will probably never know.

Macular degeneration takes your central vision. This is what we see directly in front. Glaucoma starts at the edge of the peripheral vision. This is what you see to the sides of your visual field as you look forward. Glaucoma can take all of your sight if not detected early. If not detected, a person could wake up one morning, completely blind. This is why I encourage anyone and everyone to get their eyes tested by an ophthalmologist regularly. Early detection is the key to stopping many diseases, and not just eye diseases. Macular degeneration and glaucoma are two of the four major eye diseases. The other two are Diabetic Retinopathy, and cataracts. Most eye diseases are generally not painful, with the exception of glaucoma, which some types can be extremely painful at the onset.

Macular degeneration is the leading cause of blindness in the United States. There are more cases of macular degeneration than glaucoma and cataracts combined. Diabetes is prevalent in the United States, and growing at an alarming rate. Diabetes can cause cataracts, glaucoma, and most importantly, damage to blood vessels inside the eye, a condition know as diabetic retinopathy, caused by unusual growth of blood vessels of the retina, which can leak and cause damage to the macula, much like the wet form of macular degeneration. This blood vessel leakage can cause scar tissue to grow that can pull the retina away from the back of the eye. This condition, called a retinal detachment, if left untreated, can cause blindness.

Cataracts are a clouding over the lens, which is behind the pupil. It reduces the amount of light going to the retina. Vision is blurred and reduced. The cause of this condition can be from many conditions; the most frequent cause is the natural aging process. According to the National Eye Institute, you do not have to be a senior citizen to get cataracts. People in their 40s and 50s get them. However, during middle age these cataracts are small and do not affect vision. It is after age 60 that most cataracts steal vision. Other causes may include injury, chronic eye disease, and other system-wide diseases such as diabetes. More than half the people over age 65 have some form of cataract, which can develop in a few months to several years. Surgery is required for treatment of a cataract. The diseased lens is not treatable with medication. The lens is replaceable with an artificial lens. This is a surgical procedure, frequently performed at the doctor's office. It is one of the most common surgeries performed in the United States. Over 1.5 million Americans have cataract surgeries each year.

With the exception of cataracts, these eye diseases are generally treatable. With early detection, it may be possible to slow or even stop their progression. Damaged eyes are not restorable to the condition they were in prior to being diseased or injured. Macular degeneration and diabetic retinopathy seem to have the best chance of being prevented by diet, and not smoking. I am not only a smoker, but I seldom ate foods containing the most beneficial nutrients for eyes. According to Dr. Michael Smith, MD, there is evidence that there are combinations of vitamins that may help prevent macular degeneration. Diabetics require close monitoring of their blood sugar levels and diet just to keep alive. Diabetics need to keep their blood pressure as close to normal as possible. High blood pressure increases their risk of eye disease. There are no preventative measures for glaucoma or cataracts.

I am touching on these eye diseases lightly to give you an idea about what they are and what they do. You can get detailed information from books on the specific disease, or go to the website of the National Eye Institute, National Federation of the blind, or the American Foundation for the blind. There are many other eye diseases and conditions, and some of them can lead to blindness or vision impairment. If you have an eye disease that will leave you visually impaired and with low vision, then think about this: Low vision is better than no vision. It is much easier to adjust to low vision than to total blindness.

Unfortunately, we do not get a choice of eye diseases. There is no selection menu. You have to accept what you get, and make the best of it. For some, living with low vision, legal blindness, or both become a disability that is difficult to cope with. Others consider it an inconvenience they have to deal with on a daily basis, complete with all of the irritations and frustrations that are part of living with this problem. I consider my legal blindness to be an inconvenience and annoyance rather than a handicap. Yes, I have lost a lot of the independence I once had, but I will not let it be a disability. I will not allow it to consume and destroy my life. I have too much left to do with my life, and probably not enough time to get it all done. It sometimes seems the older I get the more things I find I must do. Writing this book became one of them. I felt obligated to help those who follow me into the world of the visually challenged. Perhaps when I run out of things to do, then my time will be up. Low vision can slow you down, but it cannot stop you.

Chapter 5
Independence

Perhaps I should call this chapter, *The Loss of Independence Day*. It is not a day anyone celebrates when faced with it. There are no picnics and fireworks on this day.

I am going to devote a short chapter to this subject, as it is one of the more serious side affects of blindness. I have used the word independence a lot, as I am sure you have noticed.

For most people who are losing their sight, there comes a day when they lose a big chunk of their personal independence. Most can probably tell you about when it happened to them. I remember when it happened to me. It would have been somewhat ironic if it had happened on July 4th, but it did not. It happened on October 19. What most people do not know, is that a growing number of Americans are losing their Independence from blindness. According to the National Eye Institute, one out of every 28 people over the age of 40 is blind or visually impaired. The growing number of the so-called baby boomers is swelling these ranks. Projections indicate that these numbers shall be rising dramatically.

The people who are losing their independence are not going into bondage or slavery. These people have lost the freedom to do things or go places when and where they want to, and to do it by themselves independently. The people that I am referring to are those with low vision, a condition acquired from a visual impairment. These people, for the most part, are unnoticed by most, and all too often, their needs are misunderstood or ignored. It is easier to stick them in a corner and forget them. This group is growing at an alarming rate, and may double by the year 2020. According to the National Eye Institute, blindness affects 3.3 million Americans age 40 and older. This figure has been projected to grow to 5.5 million by 2020. The year is an interesting number on its own. 2020 (20/20?) has a little extra meaning to those of us whose visual acuity is less than normal.

With the loss of sight, there often is a significant loss of personal independence, and quality of life. Most of the personal freedoms and choices that most take for granted are lost or severely compromised. The loss of mobility can be a devastating loss. It takes a lot of adjustment and adaptive changes to adjust to and live with this lost mobility. It takes a lot of work and determination to cope with the physical and emotional challenges. Once you realize this is possible to do and that you can do it, things start sliding into place. Keep that positive can do attitude. It makes everything much easier.

Vision loss can occur rapidly from an injury or a fast moving eye disease, but is more likely to happen slowly over several years. Often, the person does not realize, or recognize that their sight is diminishing. Some refuse to admit they have a problem. This latter group poses a danger to others, as well as to themselves. Often, they continue driving and operating machinery or equipment they should not. Many are unable to read road signs or see small children in the street. With the aging process, their reflexes slow as well. These people are aware that if they cannot drive, they will lose their independence.

I remember when I made the decision to stop driving. It was one of the more painful decisions in my life. I truly enjoyed driving, going places and being able to participate in various activities. My vehicle was like a good friend I could depend on to take me where I needed to go, and when I wanted to go. It was a big loss to me at the time, and still is. I have adjusted and by planning ahead in order to arrange for transportation, when needed, I am able to do most things when I want or need to.

A few months before I stopped driving, I realized there would be a day when I would have to stop driving. I had a particularly bad form of an eye disease that was progressing and taking my sight at a faster rate than I had anticipated. At one time, I was unsure if I should be driving, but I continued anyway. This was probably when I should have stopped driving. Then one morning I came close to having an accident, and knew it was time. I could no longer put it off. I did not want to hurt anyone and realized I would be the one at fault if I did. I was an accident just waiting to happen! Looking back on it now, it had become a matter not of if, but of when it would happen. When I stopped driving, I found it to be an enormous relief, while at the same time I could see my independence disappearing, which made it a sad day for me.

To someone who has been fiercely independent most of his life, this was a major change. I suddenly had to start depending on others. I would learn to ask for help and perhaps just as difficult, to accept help when offered. This is not as easy to do as it sounds, as I had always thought asking for help was a sign of weakness. I now realize what faulty thinking that was. I believe I inherited this faulty thinking from older generations. It seems we carry more baggage from our childhood than we realize.

Many people and organizations have the desire, ability, means, and qualifications to provide assistance and training to people with a visual impairment or are in the process of losing their sight.

A person who loses their sight, loses more than their independence, they often also lose a lot of self-confidence and self-esteem. Some begin to question their self-worth, as well. These are restorable with training, helpful visual aids, and the support of family and friends. No one can restore sight to damaged eyes, but anyone can help a person deal with low vision problems, and this includes others with low vision, or even no vision. People living with blindness or a visual impairment are particularly qualified to lend help and support. They should have the desire to help and experience to be of assistance.

The loss of personal independence is not limited to people who are losing their sight. Many other physical disabilities prevent people from having the mobility they once had. One example of this would be people who have suffered a stroke, and even those with fragile bones from osteoporosis. There are, of course, numerous other conditions and diseases. Many of these make it difficult, if not impossible to enjoy the independence most people take for granted. Many of these people withdraw from family, friends, and activities. Some become shut-ins by choice, but most are from circumstance.

Most of us know, have known, or will know someone like this. A friendly face or voice on the phone can be a big boost to them. Just knowing someone cares about them can cheer them up and perhaps even give them desire to get out into society again. If you see this starting to happen to you, and are aware of this, make corrections fast. You may have to force yourself to live a normal life, whatever that is. Sometimes I wonder if I am normal, or even if I really want to be.

Becoming a shut-in by choice, serves as an indicator you do not want to deal with your problem and move forward. Depression may be creeping in or perhaps already has set in. Push the panic button and get help!

I have talked a lot about this independence thing. It probably sounds like no big deal at this point, but believe me, it will become a very important issue as your sight diminishes. Do not think you can go it alone. At some point, you will not only need help, but you will have to ask for help. You will have to accept help and learn to depend on someone other than yourself. For some reason, this was difficult for me. Once I got it through my thick skull that I had to ask for help occasionally, and was able to appreciate the help I received, it became easier. Those who offer and give help would not do so if they did not want to. They get something in return. The knowledge that they have helped someone and the good feeling which comes when they do. You may not only be helping yourself, but someone else too. This may be a strange way to look at receiving help, but it is an honest one. Do not forget that you may be able to help someone else as well. A useful suggestion or even a kind word can do wonders for someone having trouble coping with an adverse condition or situation they are having trouble living with.

On the other side of the coin, do not let yourself get too dependent on others. You have to do things for yourself, and often by yourself. It is fine if you really need the help, or if there is something too dangerous for you to do on your own. A little common sense can usually guide you here. Misguided pride sometimes gets in the way of common sense, or good sense.

Depending on the severity of your eye disease,

and how much of your sight is lost, you may be able to do many things. There will also be things you will not be able to do. For example, you may have to stop driving, but remain able to ride a bike and walk unassisted. With 20/800 visual acuity, I have no problem walking places, although riding a bike is probably not a good idea.

Sometimes you just have to experiment to see what you can or cannot do. There will be things you should not do, even if you can. It is good to know the difference. Capitalize and improve on the things you are most comfortable doing, and practice, practice, practice the things you need to improve.

Low vision may slow you down, but it does not have to stop you. Life goes on, and so must you. Others will still depend on you, as well as appreciate and admire the things you can accomplish. Do not sell yourself short is a cliche that comes to mind. I believe we all under rate ourselves, and our capabilities to do a great many things. Many of us will never know what we can or cannot do, until we try.

I once heard that life is a series of choices. As you lose your sight, you will lose some of your independence. You, yourself, will influence how much you lose. How much independence are you willing to give up? How dependent on others are you willing to become? If you are feeling sorry for yourself, you may want others to do a great deal for you. You may think this may be a good time to unload some of those responsibilities onto someone else's shoulders.

I suggest you do all you can to maintain as much of your independence as possible. Sure, you will have to give up some, and you will have to ask for help from time to time, but you are still you. Those who know you, like you, and love you, probably do not want you to change and will want to help you all they can to help you keep your lifestyle and quality of life the same. You are losing your sight, not your life. As I told someone who was feeling bad about my sight loss, and was feeling sorry for me, I said, "I've lost some sight, I'm not dead!"

It has been a new challenge, and although it has not been without its irritations and frustrations, it has been interesting and actually kind of fun learning how to live with reduced vision, while learning new things and new ways to do old things.

"Things" encompass a wide range of physical and emotional subjects, and for the most part, will need addressing. You cannot ignore them. They will not go away and come back another day. If you do not, your self-confidence and self-esteem will suffer. Without these, I do not believe you can make any kind of progress.

Chapter 6
Cheer Up!

Losing your sight is not all bad news. Forget all of the doom and gloom stuff. As hard as it may seem, there is a good side to losing your sight. When I sat down and started adding up the good things, I was surprised at how many there were. It sure made losing my sight more tolerable, not that I would trade it for any or all of the "benefits" I have discovered.

One of the things in the bigger picture is that you are not alone. You do not have to bear the burden of losing your sight, and having to deal with it all by yourself. I had thought I would have to. Man, was I wrong! The American Foundation for the Blind says that every seven minutes, someone in America will become blind or visually impaired, and as I said earlier, the National Eye Institute says there are approximately 3.3 million Americans over the age of 40 who are living with blindness. By 2020 they project this number will grow to 5.5 million. I am only using these statistics to make a point, and that point is you are not alone. You are not the first person to lose some or all of their sight. You are certainly not going to be the last.

You will probably meet many new people and make new friends while learning to live with low vision, or no vision. Many of them will probably be in the same boat you are in and will help paddle the boat in the direction you need to go. You can gain a lot of knowledge to help you deal with your vision loss from their experience. There will probably be low vision specialists to help you, with whom you will probably form lifelong bonds. All of these people will be beneficial in helping you maintain or regain your self-confidence and self-esteem. Self-confidence and self-esteem are two things I had never thought about, but which as it turns out are very important to our well-being. They are grossly underrated and affect the way we think and do things more than I had realized. Depression is a poor substitute with which to replace them. Having self-confidence and positive self-esteem are two very good antidepressants in my nonprofessional opinion.

Okay, making new friends and learning new things are good. What else could possibly be good about going blind, you say?

I have found financial benefits. Some almost seem like rewards, but they are not. They do, however, help to live a more normal life and pay the bills.

If you drive, you will have to stop at some point, if you have not already. If you are single, you may want to stop driving your vehicle (or vehicles). If you are married, you may have two vehicles. You probably will need but one after you cannot drive your vehicle. Just think of the potential savings here! You will be able to eliminate, or substantially reduce your insurance premiums, gas expense, repairs and maintenance including tires. If you are an environmentalist, think of all the good that will come from this, as well. No vehicle means there will be no payments. The money saving potential here can run into the thousands of dollars. If you have to sell one or more of your vehicles, you will probably end up with some extra cash from the proceeds.

In most areas, people who are blind or disabled may receive a tax reduction, or exemption on personal property taxes. This normally applies to the home you own and live in. For me this amounted to a $500.00 reduction.

On your federal income tax, you may receive a blind exemption of $1,190.00, and this is in addition to your personal exemption. You have to be legally blind to get these and will have to give proof. If you like to fish, most states give a reduction in license fees. In my state, I can obtain a sport-fishing license for twenty-five cents. Often there are reductions in fees for tickets to various events, and some merchants may provide discounts for merchandise or services.

In no case, could I find advertising or notices that any of this was available. You will have to seek it out and ask for it, and probably prove you are legally blind or handicapped. This can be a little tough if you are not used to asking for help, but seek, and ye shall find, and perhaps ask and ye shall receive. Do not let your pride get in the way.

I am talking about cold, hard cash here. Money you can invest in visual aids to help improve your quality of life and your ability to accomplish tasks. There are a lot of good and useful low vision aids and devices, but as you will find out, if you have not already, many of them are a little pricey. The money I have saved and/or redirected to help me live with my vision impairment has certainly cheered me up as I found them. I hope it will cheer you up too!

As my vision diminished, I noticed that my impulse shopping had come to a grinding halt. If you cannot see it, you probably will not buy it, I reasoned, but I know it was more than that. I have always enjoyed going into a hardware or auto parts store. If I could not come up with a reason to go to one of these stores, then I believe I would invent one. If they did not have what I actually needed or wanted, I would still find something I thought I needed. I seldom left empty handed or with a full wallet. After I had to quit driving, I could not go to these stores easily, and when I went into one, I could not see most things. If I could see it, or figure out what it was I was looking at, then I could not read the price tag. I need to know how much something is before I will buy it. Unless I really needed something, I would not bother a sales clerk to tell me the price. I seldom go into a store anymore without my wife. She is my primary source of transportation, and helps me find or pick out the things I need, and can tell me the prices. With all of the money I am saving, I should be independently wealthy, but it would be a good idea not to hold your breath until I am. Apparently, I must not have spent as much money as I thought I had, as not one business has gone out of business since my sight went south.

I have also found nonmonetary benefits are valuable, to me at least, and may become so to you too, as you discover them. You are on your own if you like and want to try out some of these so-called benefits. I am not recommending or encouraging you at all on this subject.

My honey-do list has gotten a lot shorter, even though I still enjoy doing, or at least trying to do many of the household chores and repairs that come up from time to time. Some things I can do and some things I cannot do. I should not do other things. This is where experience and even common sense is useful. Using common sense is, for me, often easier said than done. All too often, I ignore common sense in favor of what I perceive to be a better way, which frequently, if not usually, turns out to be the wrong way, if not a total disaster.

I am beginning to listen to that little voice in my head warning me not to do something stupid. I must confess I sometimes use my visual impairment to get out of things I really do not like to do in the first place. I almost feel guilty about doing this. The key word here is almost. There are a few things others know better than to ask me to do. Among these are such things as painting (particularly the trim), dusting, cleaning windows and pulling weeds. Painting was never one of my favorite things to do, and I had a hard enough time painting without painting areas I should not. Painting the trim around a window, or painting molding was an invitation for disaster. I cannot tell when the windows are dirty. I also cannot tell when they are clean. If you like your windows smeared or streaked, then I am your man.

Much the same applies to dusting. As to shopping and dancing, I now have a little better excuse for not doing. I conveniently forget that completely blind people do these things. Certain other chores I sometimes try to whine my way out of. Sometimes it even works! Seriously, though, I do not use my vision loss as a crutch. If anything, I probably do many things just to prove I still can. I am not sure if I am trying to prove it to others, or to myself. The satisfaction I now get from doing some of the tasks I used to take for granted I could do, is sometimes immeasurable. Unfortunately, for me, I received training to wash dishes while getting blind rehabilitation training, and I blabbed about it when I got home. Guess who does the dishes now!

This probably makes me sound like a lazy person, and perhaps I really am and do not know it, or just do not want to admit it. There are many things I do, or at least try to do. I do get a sense of accomplishment when I am able to complete some tasks. I still enjoy a challenge and being able to complete the task I am working on. The more difficult the task, it seems, the greater the feeling of accomplishment. Writing this book is one. I am enjoying writing it. If this book only helps one person to deal with their vision loss, I will consider it a success. Had I not gotten the eye disease I did, and had not lost so much of my sight, I would never have considered writing a book about anything. Add to the fact I am turning into a senior citizen, and you might wonder if I am completely sane, or perhaps a little too over the hill to be starting a project like this. According to Will Rogers, he did not think he was over the hill, because he had not reached the top yet. I say if I am over the hill, then look out below, because I am picking up speed!

Keeping a positive attitude is necessary as you lose your vision. With a lemon, you can make lemonade, and remember, there can be no rainbow without a little rain. There is a good side to most things if you look hard enough. Losing your sight does not have to be a negative influence on your life, unless, of course, you allow it to, or even want it to. Some people enjoy the sympathy and attention they receive. They do not get it for long if they are not trying to help themselves.

Let us review what I have found to be positive aspects of my sight loss.

Learning new things has been interesting and rewarding. If I had the motivation to learn when I was in school, that I have needed to learn about eye diseases, and living with a vision impairment, I probably would have been a straight A student. I have met new people who have helped me to deal with low vision and others who share the same problem and are successfully dealing with it. I have always been a somewhat private person, so letting others into my life was not easy at first. Now, I welcome new people into my life, which is another good thing. I learn a lot from each one of these positive influences on my life, with their thoughts, views, suggestions, collective wisdom, and experience. We can all learn from each other.

Who does not like saving money? You do not have to lose your sight to enjoy this feature.

Some of the nonmonetary items I mentioned are, for the most part, invalid. Most of them are selfish and usually are at someone else's expense. I would suggest you do not under value the worth of your personal successes in dealing with your vision loss. There are many positive aspects about feeling good about yourself and your accomplishments.

For me, learning to cope with low vision has not been so much a matter of survival, as it has been about revival. The entire experience has revived my interest and desire to learn and, as well, to contribute and be creative. I have gained a new reason to be alive and stay alive. Instead of surviving, I am thriving. This too, can happen to you if you want it to happen and allow it to happen. Yes, you will probably have to work for it, but the rewards can benefit you and those around you. With a positive attitude and being able to see your own progress as you become comfortable living with your vision impairment, it will be hard not to be cheerful. Your family and friends, and others you are in contact with regularly, will notice. It is contagious, and you may find yourself cheering up them as well.

Be optimistic about finding a cure for your eye disease, or a way to restore your lost vision. Millions of dollars each year are dedicated to research to find cures and treatments. Since I was afflicted with my disease, much medical and technical advancement has become available to help those with eye disease or damaged eyes. There are now treatments that will slow or even stop the progression of some eye diseases.

New low vision aids are constantly under development. Improvements to enhance existing visual aids are also under development to upgrade their predecessors. Visual aids help to enhance the sight of those who have some usable sight left and may improve it to be more usable. Sight that has been lost is not restorable at present, but there is hope that perhaps through stem cell and other research, there may one day be a way to restore lost sight.

Do not ever give up hope that medical science will find a way to restore your sight (and mine too). Do not give up on yourself or your ability to live with a visual impairment. Be happy you are alive and able to function. You can be sure your family and friends are glad. The more successes you have in dealing with the problems you are likely to encounter, the more your self-confidence and self-esteem will grow. This should translate into a happier and more cheerful you. Probably there are others worse off than you. So, Cheer-up, it is not the end of the world! It is the beginning of a new world, or at least a different world, for you. It can be interesting and even fun exploring this new world. Embrace this new way of life; it may be the only way to cope with this major change in your life. Change can be a good thing, if you allow it. You can lose your sight without losing your vision about life.

Chapter 7
Support Groups and the Role of Family and Friends

As you may remember, I recommended you find a low vision support group. A support group can help provide you with information and good suggestions on how you might handle a particular problem or situation, and can be a source of information on living with low vision on a day-to-day basis. A group can provide a lot of moral support as well. A little encouragement can go a long way. If there is no group in your area, consider forming a group yourself. Try finding a local Independent Living Center or health department to help you find a few others with low vision. You may have to post notices on bulletin boards and contact local churches and service clubs, such as the Lions International, who are very interested in helping those with low vision and the blind. You might also try to find a state department of vocational rehabilitation. These folks work with people with disabilities, which includes vision impairments and blindness. Once you have found a few people, the group should grow on its own. Word of mouth is very effective. You can contact the National Federation of the blind, and/or the American Foundation for the blind. They can give you names and contact information about statewide low vision support groups, who in turn, can tell you if there is a local group in your area, or where the closest one is. They should be helpful and cooperative.

The best support will probably come from your family and friends. They can, and should, play an important role in your adjusting and adapting to life with limited vision. Like you, they are probably a little dazed, bewildered, and wondering what they can do to help you. They will be your first and probably your primary support group. They will want to know what they can do to help you live with low vision.

It will be difficult, if not impossible, for others to have a clear understanding of what you can and cannot see, as well as what you can and cannot do. They cannot really imagine in their minds what the quality of your usable sight is (assuming you have some left). You will probably find it difficult to describe to them what you see and how much. I have tried to come up with a good description of what I see in a way others can picture in their mind, but have just about concluded that unless you are the one with the vision impairment, there really is no good way to describe what you see other than in somewhat general terms. Perhaps I just have not tried hard enough. I found myself not wanting to discuss it, because I did not want anyone thinking I was feeling sorry for myself. This is not a good idea, as they start feeling they should not talk about it. In my opinion, the more you talk about it, the more comfortable everyone becomes about discussing your problem and ways to help you.

I had kept my vision problem to myself, as long as I could, but there came a time when my sight had deteriorated to the point I could no longer hide my problem, or the fact I could not see anything clearly or read print. I had kept the situation on a need to know basis. I had not accepted my problem completely, and this became a problem. I think if my family and friends had a little better idea about what was happening, and how they might help me, life would have been a little easier for all of us. I wish I had sat down with them and laid my problem out and tried to explain what was happening and what might expected to happen, and then updated them as I learned more about it. You see, everyone in my life (and yours too) has a need to know. There I go again; my hindsight is working 20/20. Some things I really do have a clear vision about!

We can commiserate with someone who has a toothache, backache, earache, or headache. We can do so, because we have all probably experienced the same pain at some time in our life and can relate to it. Very few have lost their sight and had to live with low vision, or even no vision. Our family and friends will be compassionate, but they will have little idea of how to be of assistance to you. They may try to help you in the way they think you can use it, and it may be the furthest from your needs.

This was one of those do as I say, not as I do things. Most of the people in my life had to figure out, over time, how severe my vision loss was. They learned, I believe, by observing me and seeing what I could or could not do. Even after becoming legally blind, I was trying to go about my life as if everything was normal. I was still in denial, and it slowed my progress and probably put a lot of unnecessary stress on everyone, including myself.

It will be up to you to let them know what will help you. In a sense, you will have to teach them. They cannot read your mind. If you have not thought of this, or thought it would be of little help, reconsider. Sit yourself down and make a list of things that will help you function better, no matter how insignificant it may seem to you. As well, make a list of the things that irritate or hinder your ability to perform tasks.

One common complaint is that people move things and do not tell them about it. If you are used to the telephone or a coffee table being in a particular location and one day are in another location, you may stumble over the table at its new location. If the phone rings, or you need to place a call, and cannot find the phone because you cannot see it, you will be irritated. If you have an office, make sure no one reorganizes it for you. If they want to help organize it, great, as long as you are there with them so you will know the new location of everything. It will be neater, and you will know where everything is. It is nice to have a place for everything, and have everything in its place, but you need to know where the place is.

Everything you do and everything others do for you, or help you with, should be to help you lead a normal life. You will need the tools to help you do the day-to-day routine tasks needed to raise a family, keep a business operating, or your job secure. You may even want to consider a completely new career.

I was able to keep a business operating until I decided that it was time to sell it and consider retiring. I was in the tire sales and service business for 35 years. Now I am retired and writing a book, which seems like a career change to me. I have had enough self-confidence to travel by myself several times, which you should be prepared to do. It really gave me a sense of independence. I go bowling and I attend various meetings. I plan to go fishing, and I want to try golfing. (I will need a seeing-eye human for this.)

I enjoy recreational activities, and socializing with others. Without all of these things, one might as well lock themselves in their house and become a shut-in. In short, withdraw from society and become a hermit. I think I would rather be dead than live a solitary life and have no social contact or fun things to do.

As I mentioned, those closest to you (your family and friends, etc.) will be your primary support group. They should be encouraging you to do things on your own. This will help your self-confidence to grow. It is my hope they will notice your successes and accomplishments and give you a pat on the back every now and then. This will really help your self-esteem and self-confidence, which will make you want to do more and more. They should be looking out for you and your safety, but do not let them get overprotective. You have to look out for yourself and do things yourself. All of this can help improve your independence, quality of life, and peace of mind. You, your family, and friends, neighbors, work associates, and nearly everyone you are in contact with will influence how you deal with your vision loss and how well you adjust and adapt to living with impaired vision or blindness. It will be truly a team effort. You will need to put in a lot of effort and have a lot of patience. The rewards are worth it all. You will need to put a lot of effort into this project. Remember, you are the project, so do not do a sloppy job.

Chapter 8
Low Vision Aids and Devices

There are many low vision aids and devices available to help those with low vision or no vision have the ability to lead a relatively normal life. Some devices and aids can improve the quality of your life and help to improve your independence. Some may help you become creative and productive as well. They come in all shapes and types. Some are very highly technical and some are very basic and relatively simple. Most are useful, although some are more of a novelty and perhaps are more in the gadgets category. Some are expensive, and some are very expensive. Some are inexpensive, yet useful.

I will describe the more useful visual aids and try to touch on as many as possible. All are probably useful to someone. It just depends on their needs. What is useful to one person, may be of no use to another, so when I said useful, I should have said useful to me. I am not judging, although I may point out the advantages and disadvantages. While I try to be objective when evaluating a low vision aid or device, I also realize some of my evaluation is subjective.

I recommend before you purchase any low

vision aid, you try to find one you can try out before purchasing it. I have seen very neat devices that look like they would be perfect for me, only to find they were of little use to me. Not being a wealthy person, I could not just go out and purchase anything and everything I wanted or thought would help me. Another old saying is "look before you leap." Perhaps "try before you buy" would be a good saying.

A low vision aid can be as simple as a two power (2X) magnifier, or as complex as a closed circuit television magnification system to read and write under. Magnifiers can cost anywhere from a few dollars to over one hundred dollars. A closed circuit video magnification-reading machine will cost nearly $2,000 for a black and white model. A high-end color model, with many features can cost as much as $4,000. This is where getting help really pays off. A low vision specialist can be a big help.

A low vision specialist can determine what visual aids may be of help to you, and may have equipment and devices that you can try. There are now hand-held video magnifiers that will magnify up to seven times and will fit in your pocket. They can be useful if you are one of those highly mobile people who get around a lot and have need for such a device. It may be something that you really do not need; a novelty item, or as someone called them, a gadget that become a conversation piece instead of a useful visual aid. I have one or two of these, and although they are somewhat cute, I wish I had spent the money on something else that actually would have been beneficial to me or to someone else. Apparently, I am still an impulse shopper.

I am reminded here of when I was a kid, and figured I really needed a *Captain Marvel*. (Or was it *Captain Midnight?*) At any rate, I thought I really needed to have a Secret Decoder. It was available from advertising on the back of a cereal box. This gizmo also had a little compass and a whistle built into it. It was like a badge that would fit onto my shirt. Well, I bought the darned thing and found I could not find any secret messages to decode. I did not know how to use a compass, I could not blow the whistle in the house, and my dog paid no attention to it whatsoever. That turned out to be a waste of money, postage, and time. You would think I should have learned something from that experience, but apparently, I still like "neat" stuff. I guess there is a little boy still locked inside me wanting to burst out at times.

"Too fast we get old. Too slow we get smart". I don't know who wrote this observation, but unfortunately, I understand what it means all too well. It is probably a good thing I cannot see well enough to read the back of the cereal boxes, because apparently they still try to sell stuff on them.

If your sight diminishes to the point you cannot see the face of your watch, there are talking watches that speak the time to you. I have purchased them for as low as $9.45 up to a little over $50. Most seem to be closer to the $30 range. They work well, and make a conversation piece as well. What a deal. You get two for the price of one: a useful watch and a conversation piece! There are several talking products available, such as talking scales that tell you how much you weigh. When I first stepped onto one, I almost expected it to say, "one at a time please." There are talking clocks, and talking thermometers. There are talking calculators, and even talking dictionaries. There are talking tape measures, and talking microwaves. There are many other talking products. Technology moves faster than I do, and I have a hard time keeping up. Getting new catalogs and information on new products and updated older products is difficult unless you have the time and patience to track them down. A computer and the internet are very useful to do this.

There are also reading machines that will scan and read text to you. Some can save documents and books. These saved items are stored for future use. They are available to you like a tape recorder.

A word you will probably become familiar with as your sight degrades is the word tactile. Your tactile senses are your sense of touch. You will come to appreciate this sense as you learn to use it. There are many products for blind and visually impaired people with identifying marks on them. Some take the form of small raised dots or as some call them, bumps. There are products manufactured for the public with locator dots that are used by the visually challenged as well as those with good sight. If you have a calculator or a telephone, you will probably find the number 5 has a small raised round dot on it. This dot, is a locator dot, and is most useful to the visually impaired and blind. By finding the number 5 key, which is in the middle of the key pad, you will know where the other keys are, although the key pad on a push button telephone is in reverse from the calculator. I was using them without realizing it, well before I started losing my sight. These locator dots are available for purchase on small sheets of clear or colored raised dots that peel off and stick to other surfaces, as they have an adhesive backing on them. I use a larger safety orange colored dot to mark the settings on our washer and dryer, or at least the settings we use the most frequently. They are useful on computer keyboards and other equipment you may use. Perhaps Identification Dots would be another name for them.

I have a set of measuring cups that came with dots to identify what each held. Four dots are for a cup. Three are for a third of a cup. Two are for a half-cup, and one is for a quarter cup. I am not much of a cook, but they have come in handy every now and then. My wife likes them, and she has good sight.

Other examples of low vision aids are such things as large print books, including dictionaries and thesaurus, calendars, playing cards and crossword puzzles. A large print computer keyboard is also made, as well as sets of large print keyboard numbers, letters, etc. that can be applied over the keys of a standard print keyboard to convert it into a large print keyboard. There are letter writing guides, envelope guides, and even check writing guides. The list goes on and on but it should suffice to say that there are many,

many visual aids available to help you accomplish many tasks, and to be able to live a comfortable and normal life, or at least as normal as you might expect or even hope to have. I have found you are the person who determines what is normal for you. You can be as normal as you want to be, this way.

I have many visual aids. Some I use a lot. Some I do not. There are some I want to obtain one day, or at least try out to satisfy my curiosity. It is too easy to become a gadget junky and end up with things you may never use. As you adjust and get used to living with low vision, you will probably reduce your usable visual aids down to a few very useful items you cannot function without, or at least think you cannot function without. I have four or five visual aids I use constantly and would be lost without them, or at least it seems like I could not live without them. I am also equally sure I could adjust and adapt to not having them. Many, if not most visual aid devices are conveniences to help us deal with a major inconvenience, and I consider my visual impairment to be an inconvenience more than a disability. I do not feel disabled, or handicapped, even though technically, I am. At times, however, I may consider my visual impairment to be a pain in the ... well you know what I mean.

Visual aids certainly make it tolerable, and easier to live with. If you think of it as a disability, it will probably become one. It does not have to be. Do not allow it to become a disability. You are too strong and intelligent to let that happen to you. If you think of your visual impairment as a disability and let yourself feel sorry for yourself, you consume too much time and energy with negative thinking, which can stop you from making any positive advancement in your need to adjust to and adapt to living with low vision. It is also too easy to fall into the depression trap.

One of the more basic visual aids, and probably one of the least considered and/or understood, is the white cane. There are four different varieties used. The Long Cane is the type most people see a blind person using. This cane is a mobility tool to feel for obstacles and drop-offs, such as curbs. The ID (Identification) cane is a way to let others know the user is blind or visually impaired. While it is similar to the Long Cane, it is shorter and lighter than the Long Cane and its function as a mobility tool is limited. A Support Cane is a stability and weight-bearing tool that will aid a person's walking ability. It also serves an identification function, as like the others, it is white. It has little use as a mobility device. There is also a Kiddie Cane, which is used by children. It is like the adults Long Cane, but designed for children's use.

Most canes are composed of lightweight material, such as graphite, carbon fibre, aluminum, or composite fibre. Mobility canes come with a variety of tips to meet the needs and preferences of the user.

I use a support cane because I have a foot I injured many years ago, and it frequently lets me know about it by swelling and getting painful, so my white cane serves a dual function for me. Due to still having some usable sight, I do not require the Long Cane for mobility.

The biggest problem I have found with white canes, is many of the public are unaware of what the white cane signifies, which is that the bearer is blind or visually impaired. Some drivers who are aware will stop and let you cross the street, but do not count on it, as I have found it to be a rare occasion when someone actually does stop and allow me to cross a street. Many do not know what the white cane means, and others just do not see it. I do not get too mad at this, as I did not keep alert to recognizing a person with a white cane when I was able to drive, nor was I aware I was legally required to give a person with a white cane the right of way. Drivers obtaining a new or renewed license should be required to know this. It should be on the drivers test. At the very least, drivers should be made aware of the white cane and what it signifies.

My white cane has saved me from walking into people, as they either move out of my way or let me know they are in my path. It has been responsible for getting me help from others to find items in a store, so I know many people do know what the white cane signifies. Frequently I am pleasantly surprised to find people asking if they can help me locate something, and I cannot remember having ever being turned down when I asked someone for help. Do not hesitate to ask for help because of misplaced pride, or whatever it is that makes you hesitate. If you are on the shy side, or fear rejection, get over it! Most people enjoy helping others. Some even have a need to help others, if for no other reason than to make themselves feel good.

Many people with a visual impairment are hesitant to use a white cane. Some think they have to be completely blind to use one. I believe they just have not come to terms with their vision loss, or do not want others to notice they have a low vision problem. Maybe their ego will not allow them to admit they have a problem. Maybe they feel like damaged goods, or they are less than perfect. I have yet to meet a perfect human being. I imagine psychologist or psychiatrist could shed some light on this. I can only guess at the reasons, but knowing how I felt early into my eye disease, I can understand a little easier than most.

When I attended the VA Blind Rehabilitation Center for training with about another dozen veterans, one of the first things they did was slap a white cane into our hands and give us mobility and orientation training. We were required to have and use them anytime we went anywhere, even if it was only to the bathroom across the hall. I seldom go anywhere without mine. It is almost like a part of me. Either that or I still expect one of our trainers to yell at me for not having it! I guess this means they trained me well. They did not have to tell me twice and it was not because I was a fast learner. I just did not like being yelled at. This, of course, was why they did.

The white canes are also a safety device for walking at night. In the US, many have red tips, as well, and usually the white and red are reflective to make the person more visible at night.

Blind people have used canes to aid in mobility for centuries. However, white canes came into being after world war I. The Lions Club International began promoting the use of white canes by blind people in 1931. This organization is still actively helping the blind and visually impaired. The white cane is a symbol of independence, and tells others you are functioning independently.

Probably the ultimate mobility aid would have to be the seeing eye dog. Although most people refer to them as seeing eye dog, the correct name is guide dog, or dog guide. Whatever you call them, they are just plain wonderful, and so are the fine people who train them. It takes a lot of love and money to train one of these fine animals. They not only get their blind person safely to where they need to go, and back, but they are very close companions and the bond formed is something to be envied and admired. I spoke to a person from Guide Dogs for the Blind, an organization that obtains, trains, and matches them to the blind person. He said that it costs in the neighborhood of $70,000 just to train the guide dog and his blind person. The recipient needs training as well. A person does not have to be completely blind to qualify for a guide dog. Regaining mobility is an important function of rehabilitation, and these wonderful animals provide the means.

Chapter 9
Rehabilitation and Training

It is hard to say rehabilitation without talking about training. Rehabilitation is the process of restoration through education and training to allow us to resume former activities where possible. It can also teach new skills that will help us successfully live with low vision. If you want to return to or stay in the work force, training can help you achieve this goal. This is vocational rehabilitation. What I call general training seems to me to help us return to society.

I was fortunate. I received both. I received help from the Alaska Department of Vocational Rehabilitation (DVR). An Independent Living Center, located in the town I live, referred me to the DVR. The Independent Living Center was in the process of forming a small low vision support group when I first went to their office looking for help. There are Independent Living Centers in all 50 states and US territories. The Independent Living Center contacted the state department of vocational rehabilitation, who assisted me in obtaining a basic computer with a vision enhancement program called Zoom Text, which enlarges the images on the monitor screen. This required a larger monitor than normally used. The standard 13 to 17 inch monitor would not handle the higher magnification required for my needs. The DVR furnished the larger monitor, the Zoom Text computer program, and they provided a person to give me basic computer training.

I had never used a computer. I owned a business, which was beginning to suffer from my vision impairment. The DVR made an appraisal of my vision loss and evaluated my needs to help determine what would help me the most. It was determined that a computer would probably help me most. As I knew nothing about using a computer, the training, although brief, was invaluable. I also did a lot of trial and error do-it-yourself training, which continues to this day. This happened after I realized there was not much that I could do to break it.

As it turned out, the computer helped me to manage my business, but was of the least value to me. The most valuable aspect of the computer was, and still is, that it allowed me to access the internet, or the information highway, as some call it. The timing could not have been better.

I had determined that knowledge was going to play a big role in how I would deal with my vision loss. I needed to learn all I could about my eye disease and obtain information that would help me live with it. The internet provided this and much more. It gave me the ability to communicate with others other than by telephone or regular mail (snail mail). In a very short time, I was able to communicate with suppliers and other business contacts, as well as family and friends. Apparently, I was one of the last, in my little world, to own and operate a computer. I joined the 20th century. There is nothing like putting something off until the last minute, is there?

I recommend a computer to anyone. Just because you or someone else may be blind or physically handicapped does not mean you cannot operate a computer. There are programs that will allow almost anyone to use one. The ZoomText program magnifies the image on the screen up to sixteen times. The one I have also has screen reading capabilities. Otherwise, it can read text on the screen to you. Two other similar programs are, Magic, and Window-Eyes. The magnification programs with speech capabilities can cost close to $600. The programs with only magnification run close to $300, although there is a screen enlarger program called Big Shot, that runs $99. This is for someone with moderate vision. It enlarges 105% to 200%. These prices were in effect at the time of writing. Check for a current price before you buy any of them.

There are also programs you control by your speech. You tell the computer what you want it to do. You can write letters, and even write books with programs that will print what you speak. Two voice activated computer programs I know of are JAWS and Dragon, but there are many others on the market. A low vision specialist would be a good person to help you decide which would work the best for you.

Searching for information on the internet is interesting, fun, and rewarding. Do not write it off as too hard to learn to use. You do not need to be an expert computer whiz to operate one. My computer skills are at best, minimal. If I get in trouble and need help, my telephone and the yellow pages are available to find help.

The assistance I received from the DVR was very helpful, and very much appreciated. The computer was a perfect companion for a closed circuit television (CCTV) magnification machine that allowed me to read and write. It would magnify newsprint up to 54 times and allowed me to view small objects under it. There are many brands and types of these. I was able to keep up with the load of paperwork a small business has to contend with (big businesses too). The help I received from the DVR made me realize I needed a great deal more help if I was to continue operating a business and live with low vision. I continued my search for information. Knowledge proved to be the great equalizer in this battle.

With the larger screen and the Zoom Text program installed in the computer, I could see what I was doing. I was able to use a word processing program to write letters and email messages. I could not use my old-fashioned typewriter, as I could not see what I was typing. Thanks to the word processing feature, I was able to write (type) this book. To say I am grateful and enthusiastic about the computer would be an understatement. I will never be a computer whiz, but as long as I can get by with what I know, I will never be without one. The computer is one excellent tool.

What happened next would have an even larger

impact on my life, and my ability to cope with my eye disease. Life started being a lot less complicated after finding this valuable source of help.

I discovered the Veterans Administration, and the Department of Veterans affairs Health Care System. I am a US Navy veteran. I served in peacetime, during the Cold War. I did not think I had any health care coverage from the VA because I was not a wartime veteran. As it turns out, I am eligible. Although the VA keeps this quiet, all veterans are covered. After getting into their health care system, I found they had 10 blind rehabilitation centers around the country. They sent me to one for seven weeks of blind rehabilitation training. This was probably the best thing to happen to me since my sight started going downhill. The quality help I received there, added to the DVR training, would be what I needed to get my life back on track and my business with it. Getting the business rolling forward was of utmost importance, as five households were depending on it as well as many loyal customers who I was determined not to let down.

The training, designed and developed for me at the VA Blind Rehabilitation Center, took into consideration my specific needs, my particular eye disease, the amount of vision loss, and my abilities and desire to learn. Initially and throughout my training, the use of tactile senses (touch) were developed. There was extensive orientation and mobility training for those with severe vision loss, but everyone received mobility training in varying degrees. For some it meant learning to use the long cane with which to walk. All others learned to use a support/identification cane.

Some crafts and woodworking skills were part of the seven-week course, as well as general living skills, including even cooking. Dishwashing was a part of the cooking class, much to my wife's delight. I am nearly an expert at washing the dishes—darn it!

I also received training to read and write under magnification using the closed circuit television, also known as a CCTV. I called it a reading machine, and have since found there actually is a reading machine. The item you want to read, or in this case hear, is read to you after being placed on a scanner. It will read back what is on the page or document. Some of these machines can store information and read it back at a later time. With the CCTV, you do the reading. The CCTV just enlarges what you want to read to a point that you can see the material well enough to read it. It takes a little getting used to, as you are constantly moving what you are reading or writing under the camera of the CCTV while looking up at the television screen (or monitor). It becomes second nature after a while. Practice makes perfect. People who watch me work under one of these machines say they do not know how I do it. This is just one of several new skills I was able to learn, and may be one of the new skills you may have to learn. It is also doing a task like reading and writing differently. This is what I referred to as doing something different, or doing something differently to achieve the same results. I enjoyed learning so many new things and new ways to do old things. It is fun if you let it be fun. If you resist change, it probably will not be much fun.

For me, going to the blind rehabilitation center was an adventure, and one from which I learned a lot. I brought new skills into my home and into my life. Without it, I am not sure what kind of a life I would have now.

Finding a blind rehabilitation center that will fit your needs may not be easy, and when you do, you may find there is a waiting list to get in. There are several around the country. Some are government operated. Some are operated privately by nonprofit organizations and some centers by for profit organizations. A low vision specialist can help you to decide if it would be good for you to attend one of these institutions. He or she may be able to recommend one and even help you find one. If you are a veteran, you would be foolish not to try to gain admission to one of these fine centers.

As I mentioned, my training program at the VA Blind Rehabilitation Center lasted seven weeks. The training sessions the students received could take from four to eight weeks, which was determined by their individual needs and learning abilities. The VA facility was always full. Each week one or more students would graduate and go home. This normally occurred on a Friday. On Monday, there would be one or more persons to take their place. The facility was like a revolving door. I mention this because you may be put on a waiting list for the facility you may wish to attend, if is determined blind rehabilitation training would be right for you. You will probably need to do some advanced planning if you decide to take advantage

If it should be determined blind rehabilitation training would be beneficial to you and you are able to attend, I recommend you take advantage. You have everything to gain and little to lose other than your time.

Most blind rehabilitation centers charge little or very little, if anything, to the person attending. You will probably be responsible for getting there and back, unless other arrangements are in place. If the financial burden is on your shoulders, you may have to plan ahead, and give yourself enough time to locate financing. An independent living center may be able to help you, even if only to help find financial help. They are a nonprofit organization and do not have deep pockets. Lions club International is very interested in helping the blind and visually impaired, so keep them in mind if you really need help. Do what it takes to attend one of these blind rehabilitation centers if is recommended. If a low vision specialist evaluates your condition and thinks blind rehab training or something else would be something you would benefit from, pay attention. Their knowledge and experience will be a valuable tool for you. The experiences and knowledge from others who have been down the road you are on, is also a good source of information. You can find this in a support group. Some may have attended themselves, or perhaps would like to attend with you.

Do not forget others with vision problems. There is nothing in the rule book that says you should not help someone else cope with his or her vision loss. You may know something that would help another, and you just might learn something in return. There is one rule in the rule book I try to live by as much as I can. It is the Golden Rule—Do unto others as you would have them do unto you. Otherwise, try to treat others the way you would like to be treated. Too many people believe they should do unto others before they do unto them. Those who think this way must be paranoid and have little or no trust in others.

I have had so much help from others I feel obligated to try to do the same. I have involved myself with organizing a low vision support group in my community, and have offered our local Independent Living Center any help I might be able to provide to any of their low vision clients. I do not know if this comes under the heading of rehabilitation, but for me it has been a part of the process. It also allows me to get out, meet new people, and strengthen bonds and friendships within the blind and low vision community. I definitely do not want to become a shut-in, although I am not a social animal.

I believe we all need human contact, so please do not shut yourself out from society, or shut others out of your life. Your family and friends will want to help you cope with your vision loss, and do not deserve to be shut out of your life. Your rehabilitation is important to them too.

Chapter 10
Stuff and Things

This chapter has no specific subject matter. There is some information that would not fit into other chapters. Some are probably afterthoughts. Some thoughts may have no bearing whatsoever about going blind or becoming visually impaired. I will try not to waste your time.

One thing I wish I had done, and suggest you consider doing, is to keep a personal diary or journal of the progress of your eye disease. You can keep track of how it is affecting you and how you are dealing with it. It might be interesting to look back on the whole experience some day. It could also provide information to your doctor that might help you, or even someone else. If you have an eye disease that has a known progression rate, you can keep track of your progress and have an idea about what will be happening to you next. It could help your doctor or low vision specialist to determine their course of action. It would help them to determine when to give a treatment, if treatable, or when to recommend a particular low vision device. If you should some day want to write a book, a journal would be a great source of information.

We all seem to have our little pet peeves. The sighted, the blind, or the visually impaired all have them. One of mine is advertisers who use words for phone numbers. For example a restaurant advertising its phone number for reservations. The person hearing it is able to translate the words into the numbers necessary to dial the business to make a reservation. For example, instead of advertising the phone number 328-4373, they might advertise EAT-HERE, I know it is done to make it easier to remember their phone number and that is fine if you can see the key pad and the letters above each number. You do not have to be legally blind to have difficulty seeing these letters. All types of businesses do this, not just restaurants. Letters instead of numbers are outdated in phone numbers and have been for several decades. Printing letters above the numbers, in my opinion, is unnecessary and telephone makers should provide numbers-only telephones.

Speaking of restaurants, many people with low vision cannot read their menus, as the print is too small. Restaurants could very easily have a large print menu available by simply taking their menu to someone with a photocopier with enlarging capabilities. The cost to enlarge their menu would be minimal, as they would not need many. Even having a magnifier on hand would be helpful for some. For some, large print and a magnifier would be welcome. I would eat out more if I could read the menu.

Most business could do minor things to make it easier for people with low vision to do business with them. Most top shelves are difficult to see stock and prices, even for someone with 20/20 vision. Those of us with extreme low vision sometimes have no idea what, if anything is on some top shelves. As someone mentioned to me, short people also have this problem.

Business owners and managers would be helping their sales and reputation by urging their staff to keep an eye out for people who have a difficult time finding products or seeing price tags. They should instruct their staff to go to the customer and offer assistance. Another word for this is service. Others might call it good business sense. There have been many times I cannot find what I am looking for, and cannot locate a clerk to help me. Eventually, I get so frustrated I leave without making a purchase. I often go to another store in hopes of finding what I need or finding a friendly store that will help me.

Perhaps merchants and other businesses are not aware that there are approximately 14 million blind or visually impaired Americans—all are potential customers. I should not complain, because I save a lot of money when I do not purchase from businesses that do not care about the needs of their customers. A little thoughtfulness can go a long way, and generally is not expensive to provide. As a retired businessperson who served the public for close to 50 years, I know the value of good customer service and good customer relations. Customers and their needs are not something a businessperson can ignore. Success or failure can depend on it. I sometimes feel like going to a store manager or owner and express my concerns, but do not because I do not want them thinking of me as being an old crank, so perhaps I have no right to complain. What I think of as common sense probably requires a Ph.D. in human relations these days. Wow, I really am sounding like an old crank!

Be careful in a crosswalk, even if you are using a white cane. Painted crosswalks are there for pedestrians, and designed to help people cross streets safely. Some drivers do see them and know they are required to stop when occupied by a pedestrian. There are too many drivers not paying attention and do not stop when they should, or have to slam on the brakes when they notice a crosswalk with someone in it. Then there are the ones who just ignore the crosswalks and anyone in them. Drivers are supposed to stop for people with a white cane who are crossing a street—crosswalk or not. Many drivers do not know what the white cane signifies and will not give you the opportunity to cross a street safely. Others ignore it. The paint on the crosswalk and the white cane will not stop a 4,000-pound vehicle, so do not think because you may have the right of way everyone will automatically stop and let you cross. I live in a small community, and even when I cross a street that normally has little traffic, I stop, squint, and listen for traffic. It can be a little scary even on a normally quiet street. On a busy street, it can be downright terrifying if you do not have the training. Mobility training is one of the big items taught by a mobility instructor and was part of the training I received at the VA Blind Rehab Center I attended. I will repeat—you should get into a rehab center if your sight has you uncomfortable crossing streets and getting around. Shopping malls can be intimidating, as well. Getting to the store in one piece and back home again is more important than what you are trying to find at the store. Mobility gives you independence and plays a big role in retaining or regaining your self-confidence, not to mention your self-esteem and quality of life.

If you have not figured it out yet, you will need a great deal of patience to be successful at coping with low vision. By now, the word frustration probably has more meaning to you. Do not let it get you down. As you become more comfortable with your loss of sight and learn to live with it, most of your frustrations should go away and be replaced by self-confidence. You may need to exercise patience with others who may not understand your particular problems. Try avoiding the irritations that can clutter your mind. Most people will probably not even be aware of your vision problem, and if they do, they probably do not know how to be of help.

Others may feel uncomfortable around you, because they have no idea as to how much usable sight you have or how it may affect you. You can make them feel more at ease around you if you talk about your problem and explain to them just what you can see and what you can do with and without any visual aids.

Sometimes others will raise their voice when

talking to visually impaired or blind people. They sometimes need reminding that you are blind, not deaf.

One little irritation that bothered me was with one of those simple little things we do most days of our life. Squeezing toothpaste onto my toothbrush became a chore. No longer could I align the two and ended up missing the brush and ended up applying the toothpaste to my hand or fingers. Sometimes I missed both completely and a glob of toothpaste ended up in the sink, on the counter, and sometimes even on the floor. One of my wife's sisters suggested I squeeze it onto my tongue. This worked fine, although I was only comfortable using this method in private. I suggested this method to others with the same problem, and only got laughs. If they ever tried it, they never said so.

I looked for a device that would solve this little problem. I looked everywhere I could think of to try to find a device that would allow me to load my toothbrush easily. The first places I tried were outlets that had products for the blind and other physically challenged people. I found nothing. I do not know why this bothered me, but it did, so I invented a simple device that screws onto the end of the toothpaste tube that works just fine. I am getting it patented, and it now has a patent pending status. I hope I can get it marketed so it will be available to help others with this minor irritation.

Sometimes when you have a problem, you have to solve it yourself. I have never thought of myself as an inventor, and I do not consider myself an inventor. A problem was there I felt needed a solution, so I came up with one.

Like writing this book, it was a fun endeavor. No one has ever told me that going blind cannot be fun. So far, I have found the experience to be interesting, educational, and even a little enjoyable at times. Perhaps this is that positive attitude I suggested you keep. It is easier keeping afloat with a life jacket, than with lead weights tied around your neck. The life jacket represent a positive attitude and the lead weights represent a negative attitude.

Others will do many things for you, and there are many low vision aids to help you live better. Only you can make things happen, or allow them to happen. What you do for yourself, will make a huge difference on your personal successes or failures. In my opinion, failure should not even be in your vocabulary.

Progress may at times seem slow, and frankly it should be slow. Take your time learning to do new things, or old things in a new way. Take tiny little steps. Slow and steady will get you to your destination faster, if you do it right. Sometimes you have to allow things to happen, rather than forcing them to happen. Do not stand in the way of your own progress. You have a life to live. Make the time count for something.

Take the time to appreciate what others do for you, and do not forget to let them know just how much that you appreciate their help and support. Your family and friends will probably be at the top of this list. Even those paid to help you will appreciate recognition and a thank you. Many of these fine people often go beyond the services that they provide. They often go the extra mile to help others.

There are national support organizations for specific eye diseases that not only will provide you with information about your eye disease, but they also keep up on current research and new medical breakthroughs. Be careful not to get overly excited about something until you understand everything. It is far too easy to get your hopes up too high, only to come crashing back down to reality. Be suspicious of any new miracle drugs or unproven vitamin therapies. If it sounds too good to be true, it probably is. Taking any unproven drugs or therapies can harm you. Always check with your doctor before trying anything new.

Throughout this book, I have been telling you of some of the problems I have encountered as my eyesight diminished. I have discussed ways I used to adapt to and live with low vision. I have also mentioned things I did not do, and probably should have, and there are probably things I left out. As I said, a diary or journal would have been of great help.

The past eight years would have filled many, many pages and saved me a lot of brain strain trying to remember everything. Anything I said to do or not to do, are only suggestions. I recommend you seek advice from trained low vision specialists before you implement any new way of doing anything or purchasing low vision aids or devices. Something that works for one person, will not necessarily work for another.

As I stated, I am not an expert at anything. I am merely an ordinary human being with an uncommon problem I am successfully dealing with. I am sure there are many things I could have done differently, and probably things I should be doing now that I am not. I think I must have done a few things right, as I am happy with my life and pleased with all the things I am able to do. I am comfortable with myself. I now know I will improve my abilities with time and a little effort.

There is little doubt in my mind that if I can successfully live with low vision, anyone should be able to. There is nothing special about me. We humans are more resilient than we realize. Live, prosper, and enjoy every minute you can.

"Life is short. Eat dessert first." This was on a table at a restaurant I ate at several years ago. It has always sounded like good advice rather than being a promotion to order dessert. Do not put off until tomorrow, what you can do today may be a rough translation. The sooner you start helping yourself and obtain the help that may be beyond your ability, the sooner you will become comfortable with your vision loss and become confident in yourself and your ability to live with low vision and having a life.

I found I do not take for granted all of what I have, can do, or plan to do. I am taking one day at a time, and I try to enjoy every minute. Perhaps the normal aging process influences this. I seem to notice and appreciate what I have as well as all surrounding me. Just being alive is a gift and privilege we should not take for granted. Try not to throw up roadblocks and barriers that will prevent you from enjoying your life. Do not let other's negative attitudes slow or stop you from moving ahead. There is little you cannot do if you put your mind to it. Most of us waste a lot of our time while on earth. Time that could be better spent improving our own life and the lives of others.

Chapter 11
Conclusion

There really is no conclusion. If you are losing your sight, or have recently lost any portion of your sight, you are embarking on a new way of life. You have much to do and much to learn. If a conclusion were necessary, this would have to be it. Life as you have known it is not ending, but it is certainly going to change. In many respects, it is just beginning. You will have to adjust to a new way of life. It can be a little scary, but it can be exciting and interesting. You are the person who can make this happen. The more you know, the less you have to fear.

How To Go Blind And Not Lose Your Mind will not restore your sight, nor will it solve all of your problems. It should help you deal with them, however and deal with them you must. I purposely have kept this book short and as much to the point, as I can. You have much to do now that you have your diagnosis. A book too long and too technical would take up too much of your time and for some might just be a turnoff. You need to get to work on your problem now. I hope you can use *How To Go Blind And Not Lose Your Mind* as a guide. As you have probably noticed, there are only a few statistics, and nothing technical. This book is for others who are losing their sight and others who will follow. It is nonscientific and not written for the medical community; although I hope it will be used as a tool to help their patients. As I found out, after leaving the doctors office (after being told that I was going to go blind), I had no idea what to do, other than to wait and see what was going to happen, and then figure out what to do.

There is no book that I could find on how to go blind. This book is not designed to do this either. I have written it to help a person deal with losing their sight and I hope it will aid in your adapting and adjusting to life with low vision.

I have said a lot of do this, and do not do that. These are merely suggestions or observations based solely on my personal experiences. As I have mentioned, I am not a doctor or a low vision specialist. I am merely an ordinary person who is trying to survive and perhaps even thrive with vision loss.

As far as I have observed, there really is no right way to go blind. I believe it to be important to obtain professional help from trained low vision specialists. As well, the experience of others who have already been down the road you are on can be useful and even interesting. Having a map of this road can help get you to where you need to go. There are often different routes to get there. Study them carefully and ask for help when you need it.

I hope I have pointed you in the right direction and have provided enough information to give you an idea as to what you may have to deal with, and perhaps some helpful ideas to assist you to deal with some of the problems you may encounter. The important thing is to deal with it. Procrastination will solve nothing, and it just prolongs doing what needs doing. Procrastinating or avoiding the problem will just make it harder to deal with. Little problems always seem to grow into big problems, when ignored. Another old saying is "do not put off until tomorrow, what you can do today."

Losing your sight is certainly not a little problem, but it will present you with a little and probably a big problem or two you will have to face head on. Whatever you do, you will not be able to ignore the fact you have a problem and will have to deal with it. You have to accept your problem for what it is and learn all you can about your particular eye disease and what it will probably do to your sight ultimately.

There are nice surprises and some not so nice surprises. No surprise is easy to deal with. If you know what to expect, you will have a better understanding of what you will have to do to deal with it. Knowledge is the great equalizer in this fight. It levels the playing field. If you know your enemy, you will be less likely to fear it. An eye disease does not have to be an enemy. While you will not want to embrace it as a friend, you can treat it as a new experience which you can learn from and grow into a stronger and better person who can adapt and live with vision loss.

You should now have a better idea about what low vision is and when it may become a problem. If you drive, take yourself off the road when you know your sight is impaired. You will lose some independence, but you can get a lot of it back with rehabilitation training, low vision aids, hard work and a determination not to let your vision loss get you down—or keep you down.

Take control of the situation and deal with it with a positive and determined attitude. Work on one problem at a time. You can adapt to and accomplish more than you ever dreamed possible. Be proud of your achievements, and accomplishments. Give yourself a pat on the back when you make a new breakthrough and do not beat yourself up when you have a failure or a setback. Frankly, you are bound to have a few. If the road seems a little bumpy, think of the destination. It will be worth the trip getting there.

Do not forget or hesitate to obtain help. There are many forms of help available. You may have to seek it out, but it will be worth the effort to find it. In my case, I found that when one door opened, there were many more doors behind it, and they opened more easily, once I got in the front door.

Low vision specialists, blind rehabilitation training and visual aid devices will help you to have a good quality of life and can help keep you employed and productive. Do not forget your state department of Vocational rehabilitation if you are having difficulty at work or have had to leave the work force. Maintaining your self-confidence and self-esteem should be high on your priority list.

Your friends and family will be a big source of help. Their love and understanding will play a big role in helping you adjust, adapt, and live with low vision or no vision. Do not ignore them or shut them out of your life. You need them and they need you. Your family and friends will be your first and primary support group, but search out a support group composed of others who are losing their sight or already have lost it. Their experience and knowledge can be very helpful in learning how to live with low vision.

Keep yourself optimistic and positive. Nothing good comes from a negative attitude. A pessimistic person once told me that someone told him to "cheer up, things could be worse." So, he cheered up, and sure enough, things got worse. I prefer "cheer-up, things will get better." Well, I cheered up, and sure enough, things got better. Turn this lemon into lemonade. You can make this experience interesting, educational and with a little effort and a positive attitude, even enjoyable.

It can be exciting at times and even fun as you learn new ways of doing things and come to realize you have more talents than you ever imagined. You can bask in the joy and pride of completing tasks and projects, and surprise family, friends and neighbors with your skills and accomplishments.

Take one day at a time and enjoy each one. Tackle one problem at a time and work on them until you are comfortable with the solution. Be realistic about your abilities. There will be frustrations and irritations you will have to deal with. Do not let them get you down. If you have a problem you are having difficulty dealing with, get help. Do not let foolish pride get in the way of your progress.

Just as millions before you have done, you too can live with and even thrive with low vision or even no vision. Your largest obstacle is probably going to be yourself and the many misconceptions and beliefs you have formed in your own mind. We often think of others who are blind or physically handicapped as being disabled. Forget these thoughts. As you adjust and learn to live with low vision, you will find you can get along just fine. Others will admire you for your accomplishments and abilities. You may even amaze yourself! You can do it! Now, get busy working on yourself. There is no time to lose. Good-luck!

Sources and Resources

In the following pages, I will list sources of information and resources, such as sources of visual aids, rehabilitation training, national support organizations, and financial aid. I will list them by name, along with mailing addresses, phone numbers, internet and/or email addresses, where available. This list will only be a tip of the iceberg. There are too many to list and I am sure I would miss some, and end up with an incomplete list. Therefore, this is an incomplete list. From the organizations listed, you will find links leading to many others. This is where a computer and the internet become so very useful and valuable. Phone calls get expensive, and writing takes a lot of time and effort. I guess this is why the term snail mail gets used. Besides, if you have already lost some sight, writing may not be an option.

Regardless of your method of communication, be it email, snail mail, or telephone, I suggest you mention what your eye disease is. In other words, give the specific name of your eye disease if possible. Also, if possible, be specific about the information you are seeking. If you are phoning, make a list ahead of time, so you know, or at least think you know, what you are looking for. This will save you and the person you talk to time, and speed up the process, which will help your phone bill too.

At the top of my list would have to be the National Eye Institute, a division of the National Institute of Health, which is the focal point for most, if not all, of the various health institutes.

The National Eye Institute funds approximately 75% of all vision research at approximately 250 clinics around the US. They have been a great source of information and have led me to many other sources of information on eye disease, and information on visual aids. While I have become familiar with many of these sources, I know there are many more. For me, it has been fun and interesting digging around and seeing what would come up. At times, it seemed like a treasure hunt. My quest for information has been enthusiastic, interesting, and time consuming. The rewards have been worth it all. I only wish I could have had this desire to learn when I was going to school. Perhaps I would have been an A student. Incentive is a powerful motivator.

You will find that much of the information you gather, will not only help you, but you will be able to pass information on to others who have an interest in coping with vision loss. These will include family and friends who can be a great help to you. Many of the sources listed in the following pages have been of great help to me in locating information on eye diseases.

(The) Glaucoma Foundation
116 John Street, Suite 1605
New York, NY 10038
1-800-452-8266
212-285-0080
Info @glaucomafoundation.org
http://www.glaucomafoundation.org

Glaucoma Research Foundation
490 Post Street, Suite 1427
San Francisco, CA 94102
1-800-826-6693
415-986-3162
http://www.glaucoma.org

Independent Living Services for older
Individuals Who Are Blind
U.S. Department of Education, OSERS
400 Maryland Avenue SW, Room 3326, MES
Washington, DC 20202-2741
202-205-9362, or check your local phone
Directory for an Independent Living Center
http://www.ed.gov/programs/rsailob/index.html

National Library Service for Blind
and Physically Handicapped
Library of Congress
Washington, DC 20542
1-800-424-8567
202-707-5100
202-707-0744 (TDD)
nis@loc.gov
http:/www.loc.gov/nis

Lighthouse International
111 E. 59th Street
New York, NY 10022
1-800-829-0500
212-821-9200
212-821-9713 (TDD)
infor@lighthouse.org
http//www.lighthouse.org

Lions Clubs International
300 W. 22nd Street
Oak Brook, IL 60523-8842
830-571-5466
http://www.lionsclubs.org (Note: There are
Lions Clubs in most Localities and services
vary from club to club)

Macular Degeneration Partnership
8733 Beverly Boulevard, Suite 201
Los Angeles, CA 90048
1-888-430-9898
310-423-6455
http//www.amd.org

National Association for Parents of
Children with Visual Impairments
P.O. Box 317
Watertown, MA 02471
1-800-562-6265
617-972-7441
http://www.spedex.com/napvi/

Resources for Rehabilitation
22 Bonad Road
Winchester, MA 01890
781-368-9094

National Eye Institute (NEI)
31 Center Drive MSC 2510
Bethesda, MD 20892-2510
301-496-5248
http://www.nei.hih.gov

National Federation of the Blind
1800 Johnson Street
Baltimore, MD 21230
410-659-9314
http//:www.nfb.org

Talking Tapes/Textbooks for the Blind
16 Sunnen Drive, Suite 162
St. Louis, MO 63143-3800
1-877-926-0500
314-646-0500
http://www.talkingtapes.org

Visions/Services for the
Blind and Visually Impaired
500 Greenwich Street, 3rd Floor
New York, NY 10013-1354
1-888-245-8333
212-625-1616
http://www.visionsvcb.org
National Institutes of Health
9000 Rockville Pike
Bethesda, Maryland 20892
301-496-4000
301-496-4000
http://www.nih.gov/health/infoline.htm

The next listings are for sources of visual aids. It is just a sampling of suppliers and manufacturers. Some of the suppliers are ones I use and some of the manufactures make products I use, or have been able to see and/or try. In my opinion, you should always try before you buy. What may work for one person may very well not fit the needs of another. A low vision doctor can assess your needs and make specific recommendations. They often have various devices you can try. Look for a business that stocks Assistive Technology products.

You can call low vision specialists, Independent Living Centers, Blind organizations, and perhaps ophthalmology offices or clinics for suggestions to find low vision products in your area. If you live in a small community, you may have to travel to a larger city to find what you need. You can order from a few very good mail-order businesses from a catalog. Just be certain that what you need is what you are ordering. Some things are not returnable once used even just once. If they have a return policy that will allow you to try out a product and be able return it if you do not like it, then go for it. Do not forget that time and effort is needed to pack and ship it back (usually at your expense).

I apologize to the manufacturers and outlets that have not been included in the following list. I recommend you search the internet for vendors specializing in technology for the blind. Once there, you will find information and links that could keep you busy for days.

Adaptive Technology Consulting, Inc.
P.O. Box 778
Amesbury, MA 01913
email: dvesely@adaptivetech.net

Ai Squared
P. O. Box 669
Manchester Center, VT 05255
802-362-3612
Fax: 802-362-1670
email: zoomtext@aisquared.com

Bartimicus Group
1481 Chain Bridge Road, Suite 100
McLean, Virginia 22101
703-442-5023
Fax: 703-734-8381
email: adapt2c@bartsite.com
http://www.bartsite.com

Clarity Solutions
320 B Tesconi Circle
Santa Rosa, CA 95401
707-526-9204
1-800-575-1456
email: clarity@clarityaf.com
http://www.clarityaf.com

Enhanced Vision Systems
17911 Sampson Lane
Huntington Beach, CA 92647
1-800-440-9476
sales@enhancedvision.com

Freedom Scientific
Blind/Low Vision Group
11800 31st Court N
St. Petersburg, FL 33716
1-800-727-803-8000
email: info@freedomscientific.com

Lighthouse International
111 East 59th Street
New York, NY 10022-1202
212-821-9200
1-800-829-0500
http://wwwlighthouse.org

LS&S Group, Inc.
P.O. Box 673
Northbrook, IL 60065
1-800-468-4789
email: lssgrp@aol.com

Magnisight, Inc.
P.O. Box 2653
Colorado Springs, CO 80901
1-800-753-4767
email: sales@magnisight.com
http://www.magnisight.com

Maxi-Aids
42 Executive Blvd.
Farmingdale, NY 11733
1-800-522-6294
http://www.maxiaids.com

pendix

Optelec US, Inc.
6 Liberty Way
Westford, MA 01886
1-800-828-1056
508-392-0707
email: optelec@optelec.com

Pulse Data HumanWare, Inc.
175 Mason Circle
Concord, CA 94520
1-800-722-3393/ 925-680-7100
http://www.pulsedata.com

ScanSoft, Inc.
Worldwide Headquarters
9 Centennial Drive
Peabody, MA 01960
1-800-443-7077
978-977-2000

Sight Connection
9709 Third Avenue
Seattle, WA 98115-2027
1-800-458-4888
206-525-5556
http//eee.sightconnection.com

Telesensory Corporation
520 Almanor Avenue
Sunnyvale, CA 94086
408-616-8700
E-mail: info@telesensory.com

Video Eye Corporation
10211 Emerald Avenue
Boise, Idaho 83704
208-323-9577
http://www.videoeyecorp.com

IN CANADA
Canadian National Institute for the Blind
(CNIB)
19229 Bayview Avenue
Toronto, Ontario M4G 3E8
416-486-2500
http://www.cnib.ca
(has offices throughout Canada
serving all provinces)